# Make (Sneaky) Art

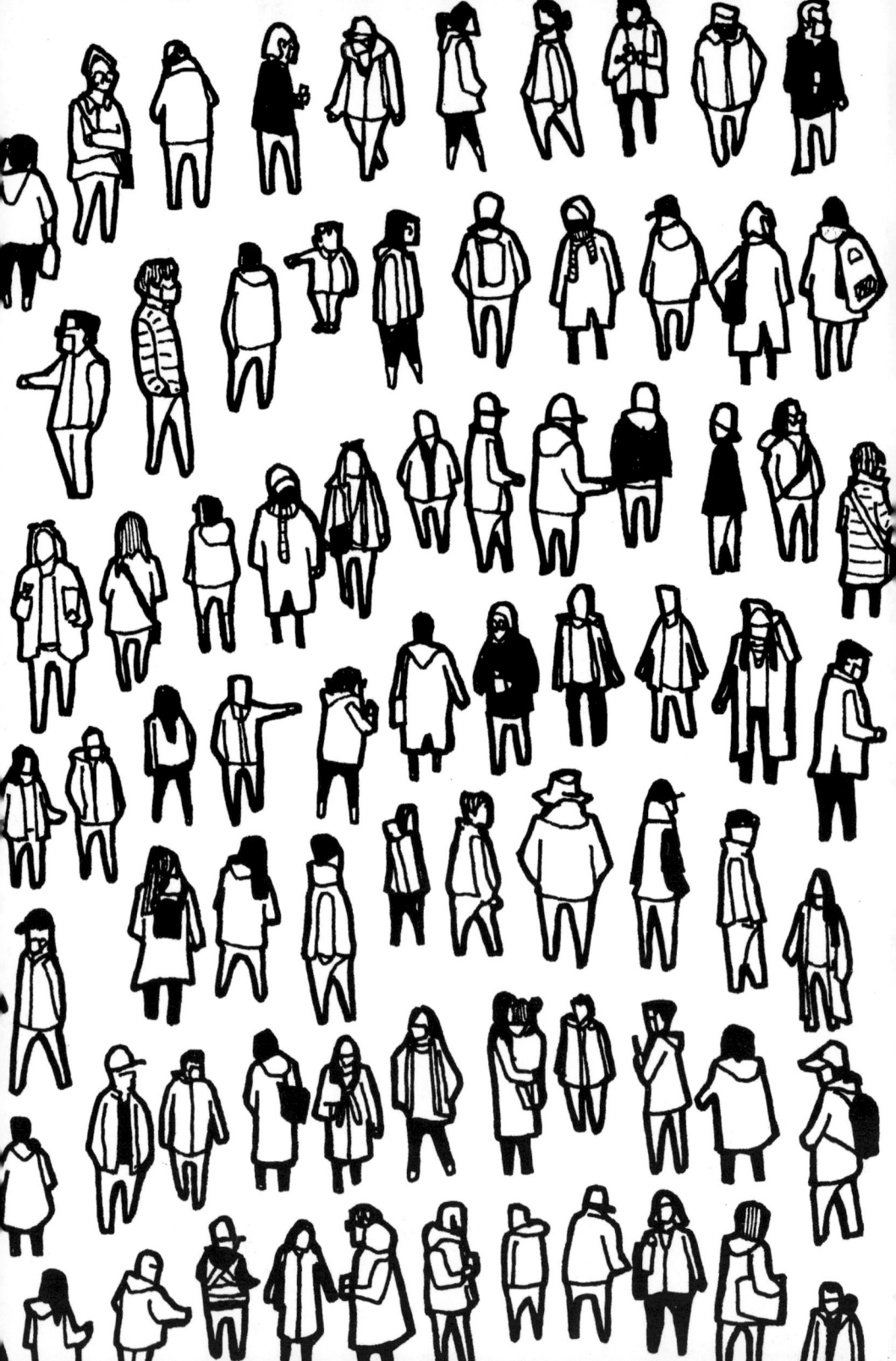

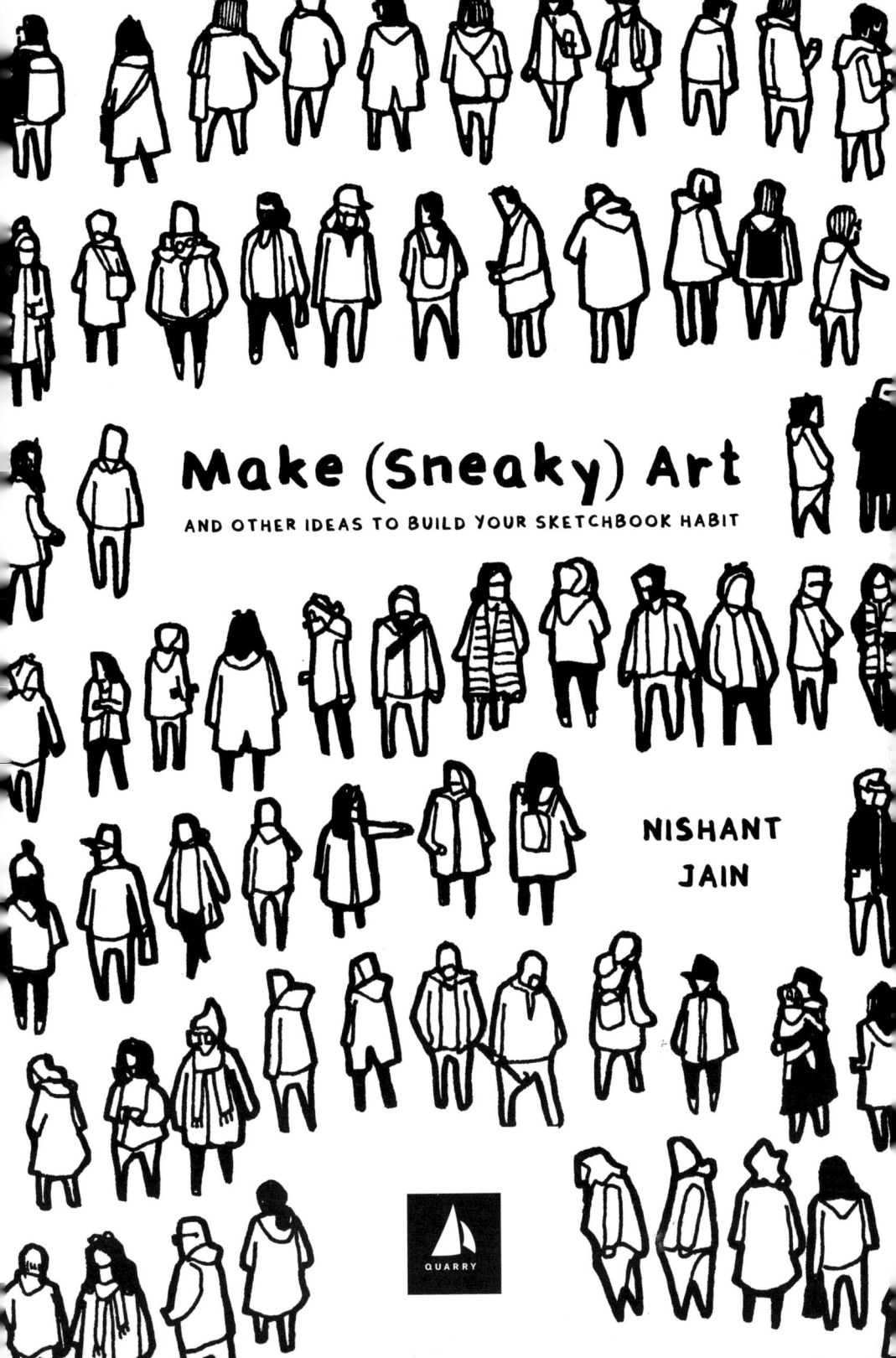

# Make (Sneaky) Art

### AND OTHER IDEAS TO BUILD YOUR SKETCHBOOK HABIT

## NISHANT JAIN

QUARRY

**Quarto.com**

© 2025 Quarto Publishing Group USA Inc.
Text, Photos, Illustrations © 2025 Nishant Jain

First Published in 2025 by Quarry Books, an imprint of The Quarto Group,
100 Cummings Center, Suite 265-D, Beverly, MA 01915, USA.
T (978) 282-9590 F (978) 283-2742

EEA Representation, WTS Tax d.o.o.,
Žanova ulica 3, 4000 Kranj, Slovenia.
www.wts-tax.si

Quarry Books titles are also available at discount for retail, wholesale, promotional,
and bulk purchase. For details, contact the Special Sales Manager by email at
specialsales@quarto.com or by mail at The Quarto Group, Attn: Special Sales Manager,
100 Cummings Center, Suite 265-D, Beverly, MA 01915, USA.

10 9 8 7 6 5

ISBN: 978-0-7603-9419-9

Digital edition published in 2025
eISBN: 978-0-7603-9420-5

Library of Congress Cataloging-in-Publication Data available

Design and Page Layout: Merideth Harte

Printed in Huizhou City, Guangdong, China TT022026

# Acknowledgments

My journey as an artist could not have begun without the decision to break away from my old life. All the good things of the decade since have been possible only because of my partner, my wife, Smita. We have a little baby now, but she is the OG baby of my life.

When I explained that I was quitting my PhD program to become a writer, both my parents and in-laws supported the decision. When the writing did not work out, they trusted me again on the new path to becoming an artist. They have cheered and supported me at every turn. I am very lucky.

All my good ideas come from other people. So I want to thank all the artists and writers I have met on my creative journey. This includes everyone in the Urban Sketchers chapters of Chicago, Minneapolis, and Vancouver, the arts community of Eau Claire, the wonderful guests on *The SneakyArt Podcast*, and the community of writers on Substack. For helping me think about writing and art and the business of writing and art, I want to thank Samantha Dion Baker, Amy Stewart, Gabi Campanario, Ellen Vesters, James Richards, Mike Sowden, and Beth Spencer.

The SneakyArt Post is welcomed into thousands of inboxes all over the world by readers who support and validate my work. My creative journey is supported by hundreds of paying subscribers who engage deeply with my work. It is a privilege to have a space in your inbox, and a share of your time and attention every week.

I want to thank Michelle Bredeson at Quarto Publishing for offering me the chance to write this book. Working with talented, dedicated people in publishing has been a tremendous learning opportunity.

My world comprises countless strangers—pedestrians on sidewalks, people in cafés, commuters on transit—who make it a rich, diverse, and beautiful place to be. It is an honor to have you in my world, and I am glad to be a tiny part of yours.

I was in the 11th grade when, during a reading of Shakespeare's Julius Caesar, I made a sneaky drawing of our teacher. He walked up behind me and peered over my shoulder to see it. I looked up nervously, but Mr. Ritchie smiled and said, "Good job." I think about that often.

# CONTENTS

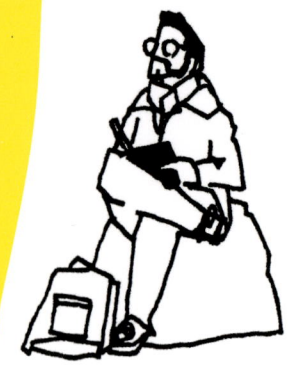

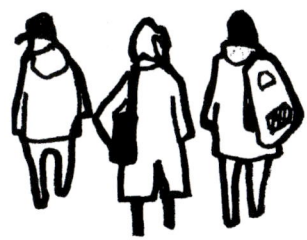

# Introduction

A few years ago, an entire lifetime ago, I sat at my desk, staring at the flickering cursor on the screen, trying to write. I had left midway through a PhD program in neuroscience to become a novelist, and I was stuck on the fifth draft of the great novel inside my head. It was the worst day of my life as a writer.

Curiously, it was also the first day of my journey to become an artist. But I did not know it then. Grabbing a pen and notebook, I went out for a walk. I was angry at the words that would not come, and I was afraid of never finding them again. Writing a good story needs you to be completely naked in front of countless strangers. Even the lies you write tell the truth about you. I realized I was not ready to do that. And I did not want to think about what that meant for my lifelong dream to be a writer.

I sat in a nearby café, watching the other patrons. People in cafés are busy in their own worlds, locked in conversations, captivated by their phone screens, tucked into a good book, expressing their lives. To distract my racing mind, I started drawing them. I was an immigrant in America then, uncertain of my environment, trying to make a home in a new world. And observing people through the pages of a sketchbook suddenly made a lot of sense. My mind was active, receptive to sounds and smells and sights around me. My body was occupied, leaning over the table, feet tapping, hands working the pen on the page. After an hour, I had a finished sketch on my page that felt great, even though it did not look all that good.

This was my first big realization about drawing, and the main reason I went back to draw the next day—that it could feel great, even if the result on the page was not very good. I told myself I would be more sneaky the next day, so no one saw me do this silly thing. *I can even call it sneaky art, ha!*

Soon after, we moved to a little town in the middle of the Midwest. In Eau Claire, Wisconsin, where there were no towering skyscrapers or historic architectural landmarks, I used my sketchbook as a crutch—to

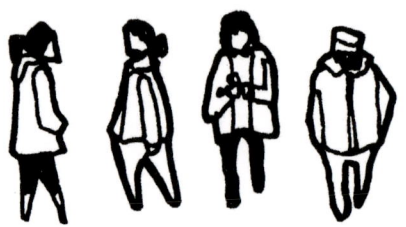

support my anxiety of being an outsider, to fulfill my need to keep drawing, to validate my decision to sit alone at the café for an hour, knowing no one at all.

Not knowing anyone in a big city is different from not knowing anyone in a town. In the city, strangers live around one another all the time, and everyone can blend into the crowd. But in smaller towns, a stranger stands out. And with brown skin and a beard, I felt particularly . . . conspicuous.

In public spaces, I looked at people so different from me, but the drawing habit helped me find commonalities. I noticed which coffee they ordered, and smiled when it was the same as mine. I overheard snippets of conversations, and in this way their world became part of mine. I observed posture and gait and friendship dynamics. The sketchbook was the tool that allowed this to happen.

Later, it helped me make friends at the café, and in this way I also found my first customers. Someone suggested I set up a tent at the farmer's market to sell my drawings. That summer at the farmer's market, I introduced my work to dozens of bleary-eyed strangers and learned valuable lessons in marketing. Convincing someone to buy art at 7 a.m. on a Saturday morning, when they only came to get some bread and cheese, is not easy. But if you can do it, you are onto something good.

Drawing in Eau Claire taught me that beauty is not limited to the big cities with grand architecture. It can be found in the everyday lives of ordinary people, in every part of the world. Sneaky Art began with the idea of the artist being sneaky, but soon I learned that the art is sneaky too. There it is, right in front of you, hiding in plain sight, waiting to be seen.

I was at a meetup of urban sketchers in Minneapolis when someone first said to me that they could recognize my work anywhere because I had my own style. I remember it clearly because I was completely stunned. Until that moment, I had assumed it was impossible for someone like me to have a style.

In my mind, style was an unattainable object, something you had to be born with, something that needed elite education or training. A self-taught amateur like me, at the advanced age of thirty, surely had no chance. But I was wrong.

Style is not a matter of skill, or education, or gift of birth. Your style is the most authentic representation of who you are on the page. Its elements—your personality, ideas, thoughts, idiosyncrasies—are already inside you. You develop your style by learning how to work with these elements. In this book, I point you to the path that will help you develop your style. But it needs you to do the walking. With a sketchbook, page by page, step by step, it needs you to observe your world and react with your curiosity.

The panopticon is a theory of social control in which prisoners police their own behavior because they believe that they are under constant monitoring. It was after my modest Instagram account blew up that I realized that social media is also a panopticon, one in which we are both prisoners and guards.

On social media, we self-monitor by means of a Like button that tells us how good or bad we are. We chase likes every day, doing whatever it takes to get more than the day before, even faster tomorrow than today, higher and higher, faster and faster. Our self-expression matters only with respect to how many likes it can gather. To get the most likes, social media needs us to present ourselves as finished products: perfect brands and desirable objects. It could be your personality that is the brand, or your physical appearance the desirable object. For artists, their work needs to be the desirable object, with themselves the perfect brand. And until it is desirable, and until we are perfect, we are too ashamed to share our arts. Often, we are too ashamed to even make our arts.

The panopticon of social media makes us smaller than we are, by training us to obey its whims, turning us into passive consumers of a feed designed by an inhuman algorithm. We must break out of this prison.

In these distracted times, a sketchbook habit helps me reclaim my attention span. The ability to ignore my phone when I am outdoors is a superpower. Noticing other people and the world I share with them grounds me to my physical environment, makes me present in the here and now. All it needs is pen and paper. I wrote this book to share how this works.

Art is all journey, no destination. No one ever arrives. No one is ever finished. And this is the most beautiful thing about it.

A sketchbook habit will, I hope, show you the joy of doing things—not for the beautiful results, but because making art is good thing to do. A sketchbook empowers you to notice what is beautiful, to think about why you find it beautiful, and to represent that beauty in the manner of your choosing. It gives you active agency in finding, interpreting, and depicting the beauty of your world. By making you better able to see its beauty, a sketchbook makes your life more beautiful.

Reader, we live in a big, beautiful world. But a lot of people make a lot of money by making that difficult to notice. A sketchbook can help you escape their vicious designs. Let this book be the start of your journey to see many beautiful things. It would be my honor to walk with you, and point the way.

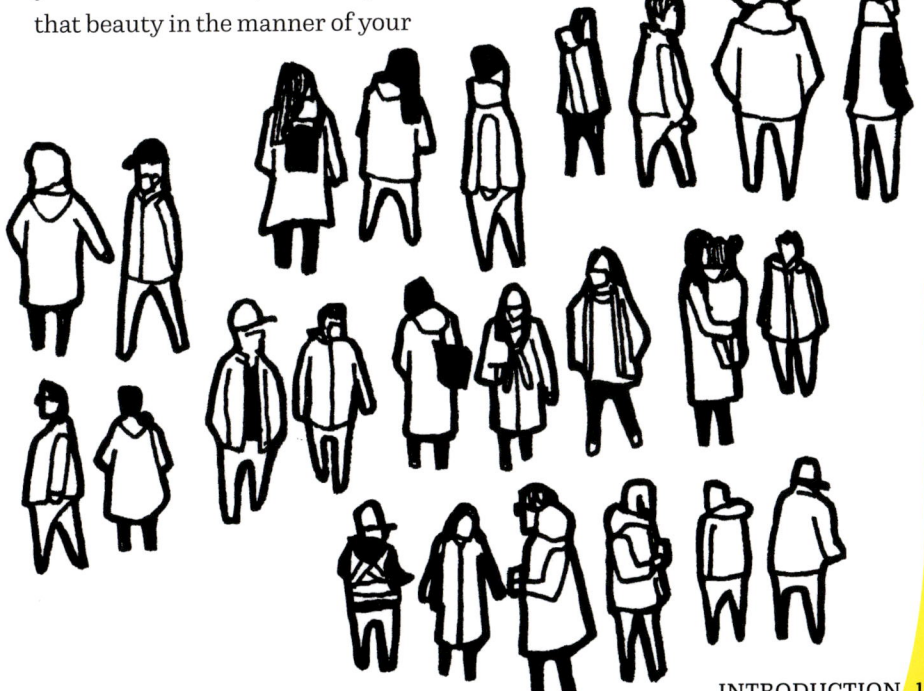

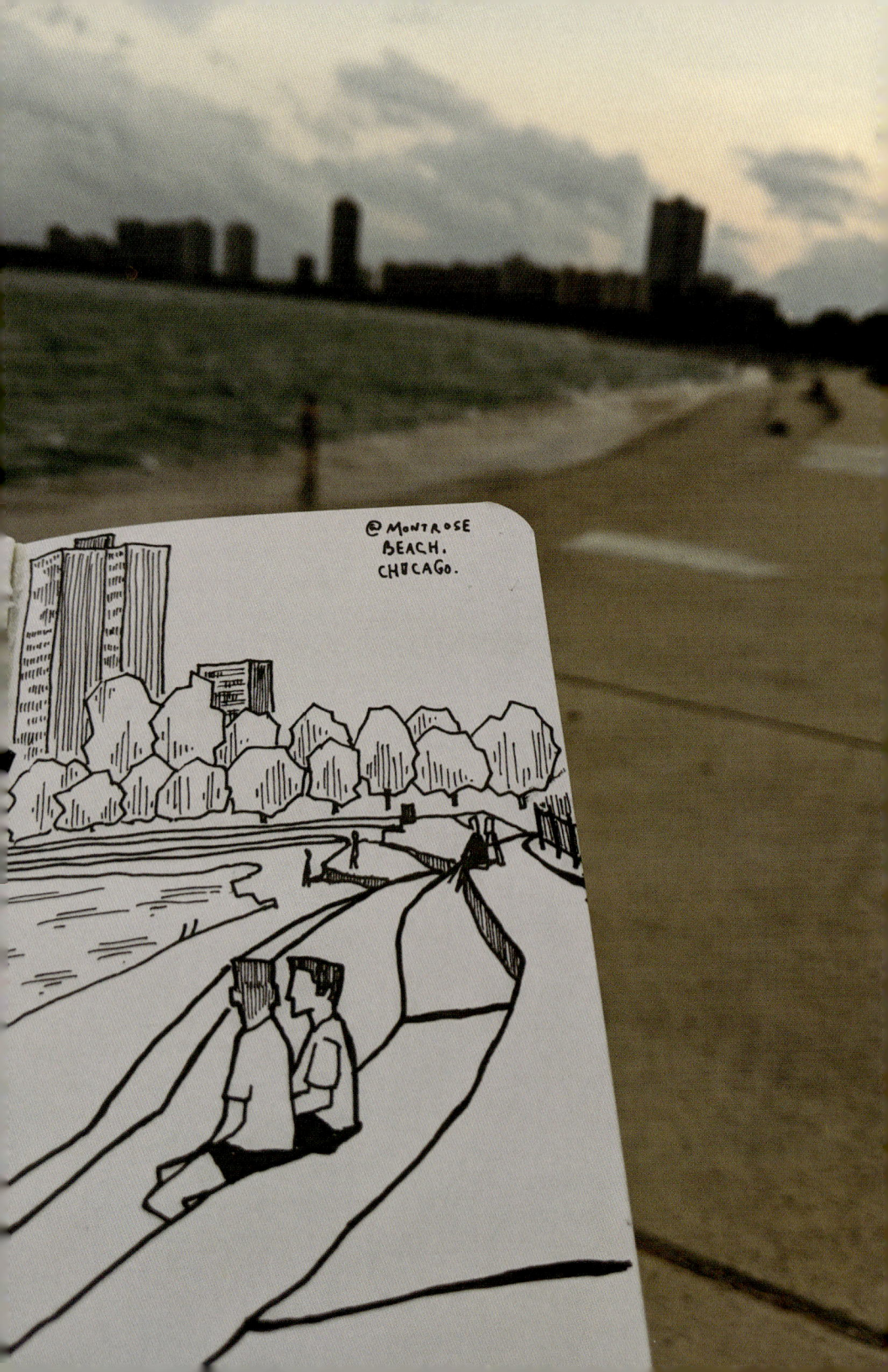

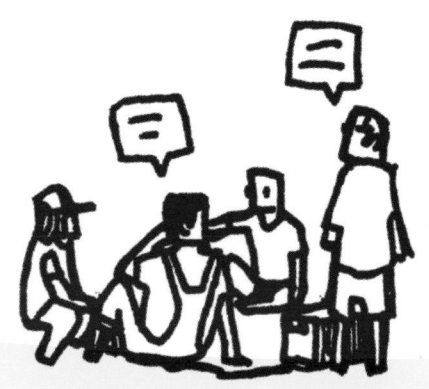

# CHAPTER 1

## WHAT AND WHY:
## BEING SNEAKY IN THE
## PURSUIT OF ART

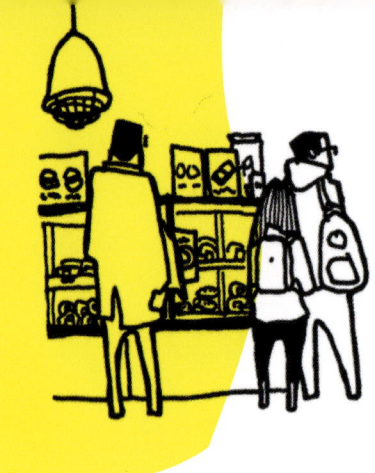

## We Live in a Beautiful World

I want to tell you that we live in a beautiful world.

Even when we do not understand it, even when it appears cruel and indifferent, even in the midst of ugliness and strife and malice. Within each of us is a capacity to recognize beauty that no one can take away from us. But a media environment designed to be distracting and manipulative can sometimes make beauty difficult, or even impossible, to find.

Today we live inside various media environments: screens, sounds, notifications, and social media feeds consume our attention span, leaving only crumbs for the things we actually want, the things that would make us happy.

The reason for this book is therefore simple: to make it easier to recognize beauty in our distracted, divided, unhappy world. To use a sketchbook habit to reclaim our attention span. To equip you with the tools that help add more beauty to this world we share.

↓ *Sketching on the beach in Vancouver*

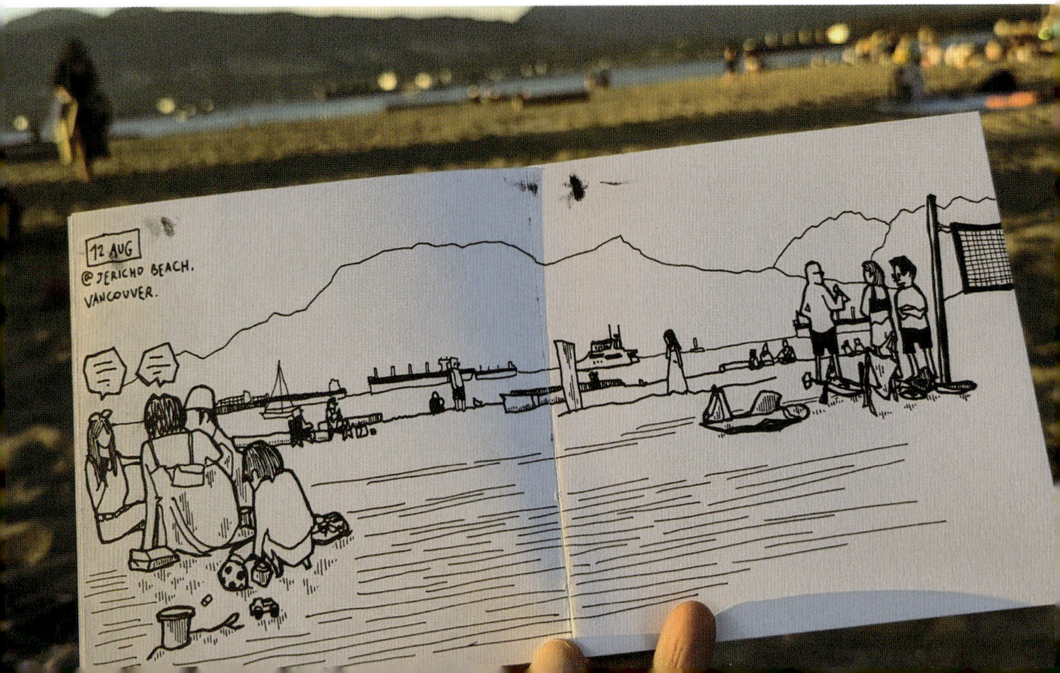

# Why I Started Being Sneaky

My name is Nishant, and I am a Sneaky Artist. This is a job title I made up for myself. Turns out, you are allowed to do that sort of thing! Not that it was easy. Before I could convince anyone else, I had to do the much harder job of convincing myself.

In the shortest version of this story, I left in the middle of a PhD program (in neuroscience) to chase my dream of becoming a writer. And I wrote and wrote until I hit a terrible writer's block. Looking for an excuse to run away from my desk, I picked up a sketchbook and started walking about drawing people and neighborhoods in the magnificent city of Chicago. I thought I was just buying myself some time, but I had unintentionally embarked on a (sneaky) journey to become an artist.

I called it "sneaky art" because I was ashamed of the situation I was in: a grown adult making terrible drawings. What would people think if they saw me? What would they think if they saw the pages? What would they say or, worse, what would they NOT say? I decided to be sneaky so no one would see me drawing, so no one would know I was even there.

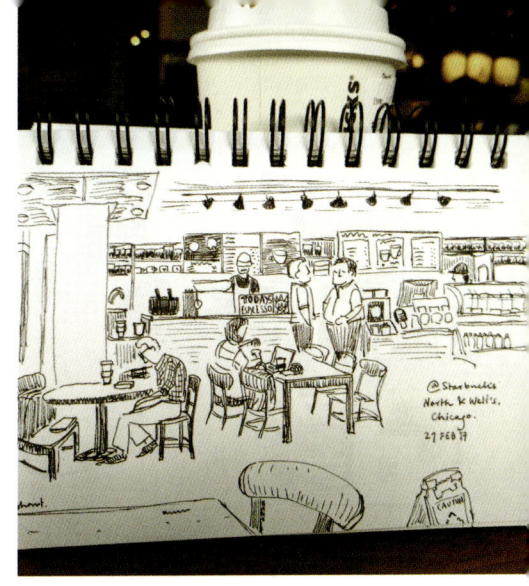

↑ *The first time I made sneaky art, Starbucks in Chicago*

I would sit at corner seats in cafés, draw into a small sketchbook with a single pen, and get out of there before anyone got suspicious. It was silly, as all self-imposed shame is. But it was also me, and I am only human, just like you. We carry shame we do not need to, and burden ourselves with unvoiced opinions and imagined ideas.

I am pleased to say I got over it. Now, here is the longer version of my story . . .

When I was growing up in India, the prevailing wisdom was to keep hobbies as hobbies, and be pragmatic about your career decisions.

Becoming an artist is an unwise decision. The world tells you in no uncertain terms that success is rare, disappointment and failure are common, and there is never enough money. *What kind of job is artist anyway?*

But if you look carefully, the world also shows you that we are in desperate need of art. Even in the darkest of times, we seek stories and songs and paintings and TV shows to uplift our spirits. Stories give us solace, songs connect us to emotions buried deep inside ourselves, and art is a magical, inexplicable connection with higher powers, with impossible worlds, with the dark depths and dizzying heights of human imagination. We need art to understand other people. And we need art to understand ourselves.

Our need to understand our world and its people and how we fit together, our need to construct world views and understand different perspectives, is a deeply human thing. So making art may in fact be the most deeply human thing you can do.

When I was young, I already knew I wanted to be a writer. But I did as I was told. Being good at science, I went to an engineering college and worked on race cars. After a bachelor's degree as a mechanical engineer, curiosity led me to human movement analysis,

and that became a master's degree in biomechanical engineering.

In the summer of 2014, I was a PhD researcher studying neuromuscular movement deficiencies in chronic stroke patients. I ran long experiments collecting Big Data on brain activity and muscle signals. I ran Big Math on that Big Data. I was on my feet all day and hunched over a desk all evening. But my little secret was still alive. There was a bluebird in my heart that wanted to get out. Science was the thing I was reasonably good at, but it did not keep me up at night. What kept me up at night was the desire to write stories.

I wrote all the time, anything and everything. I wrote short stories and poems, scripts for television in India, and made short films with friends. I drew a stick-figure webcomic that became briefly famous on early social media. Then everything changed one night at a random open mic event in Chicago.

I saw an aspiring comic do a terrible set. Five minutes of pure cringe. No one laughed, no one clapped. The comic smiled into the deathly silence and returned to his seat, and I was transformed. I had seen him before at other open mics. He was always terrible, and no one ever laughed. And he always smiled and returned to his seat,

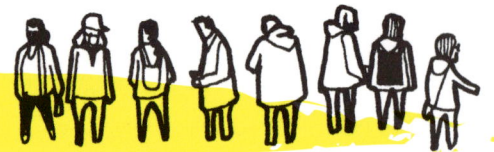

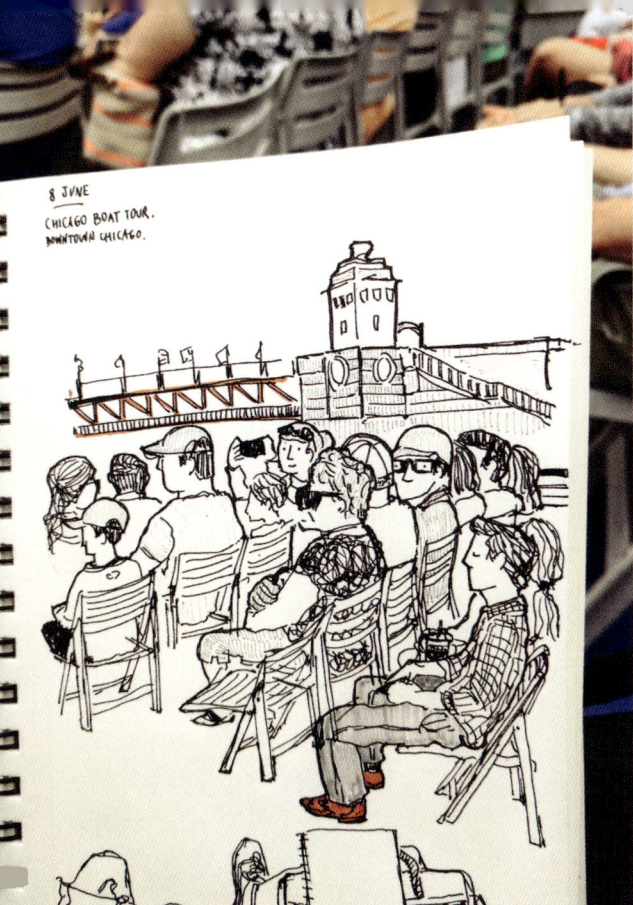

8 JUNE
CHICAGO BOAT TOUR.
DOWNTOWN CHICAGO.

← *Taking a friend on a boat tour in Chicago*

and came back with fresh material the next week. In this unfunny, yet supremely confident, person I found the inspiration I needed. *If he could do this, I asked myself, why couldn't I? How could I not commit to my creativity? What else is the point of anything?*

Maybe I was just looking for an excuse. The next week, I quit my PhD program and embarked upon the incredible journey of writing the greatest novel of all time. Along the way, I figured a sketchbook might help me learn to draw better comics. After 50,000 words and five rewrites, the novel did not pan out. But, quite accidentally, I discovered a great joy in people-watching, in deep observation, and in quick sketching. Quite accidentally, I found myself becoming an artist.

If there is a single lesson I can give you now, let it be this: do things without knowing what they will become, without expectations, and without over-planning. Just get into them. Life is more fun when it is led by curiosity.

# Good Reasons to Be sneaky

I started making sneaky art out of a misplaced sense of shame and a terrible case of imposter syndrome. But being who I am, and pushing forward despite that, was a good thing. Here are some good reasons to be sneaky in the pursuit of art:

> It can be intimidating to make art in public spaces if you are under-confident or self-conscious. Being sneaky allows you to observe without being observed, to draw without getting in your own head.

> As an immigrant in North America, I was frequently overwhelmed by the workings of my New World. When I felt like an outsider, the sketchbook gave me a reason to occupy space in a café, park, or bar. When I did not understand, drawing helped me better understand the people around me.

> A sketchbook will tell you who you are, if you let it. Making sneaky art is the invitation to keep a secret sketchbook that you do not share with other people. A secret sketchbook is a wonderful idea, because we all need safe spaces where we can express ourselves without the influence and interjections of others. A sketchbook can be the visual journal that helps you better understand yourself.

> A sneaky-art pursuit helps you see the hidden beauty of everyday life. It teaches you to look past your own cynicism and interpret your world with fresh eyes.

The art in this book will exemplify all of the points above. Flip through the pages and stop at any image that looks interesting. Ask yourself, what sparks your curiosity? What makes you stop? What makes you look, then look again?

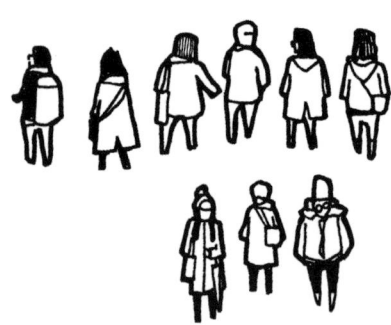

# A Toolkit for sneaky Art

You do not need much to start drawing. It could be just a simple sketchbook and one or two pens (or pencils!). In fact, a minimal toolkit is sometimes the best decision for the aspiring (sneaky) artist. To take out a full kit of colors and brushes and a big sketchbook would be inviting undue attention upon yourself. *Who is this person?* People may think to themselves. *What kind of crazy thing will they do now?*

Very un-sneaky.

But outside of the ordeal of dealing with unwanted questions, a minimal toolkit is also great for anyone who hesitates to get started. Here are some reasons why:

> **Do not waste time getting started.** Carrying only a few—but trusted—tools means always reaching for something comfortable. When inspiration strikes, we must be ready to begin!

> **Overcome decision anxiety.** Agonizing over which pencil to use, or trying to find the right color, can be exhausting. Having a small toolkit allows us to stay in the flow of creating, to go deeper in the journey, instead of constantly interrupting ourselves.

> **Creativity thrives within constraints.** A limited toolkit will fire your creative instincts! To adapt and improvise is at the heart of creative thought. Doing this on the sketchbook page can lead to fun and insightful discoveries about your art, your taste, and yourself.

> **Forgive your errors.** I started drawing with a pen because I was tired of my own perfectionism. Putting myself through several "bad" drawings taught me that the joy of finishing is greater than the joy of getting it exactly right. There is a dopamine hit waiting at the end of every page, and turning the page is a gift we get to give ourselves. A simple toolkit leaves no room to get everything exactly right, and allows us to focus on the joy of making art.

When planning your minimalist toolkit, refer to the following for some useful combinations.

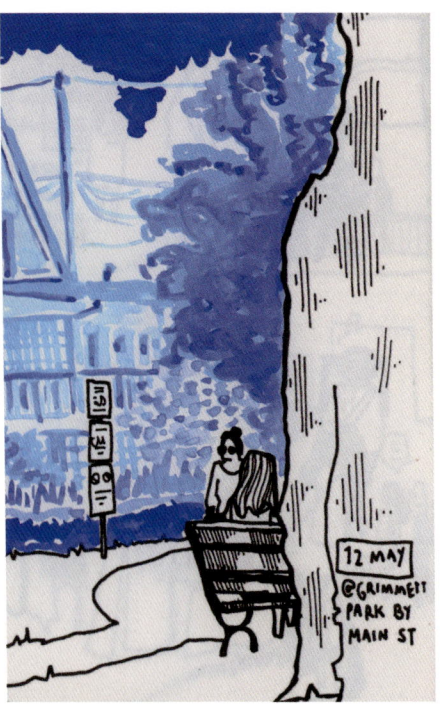

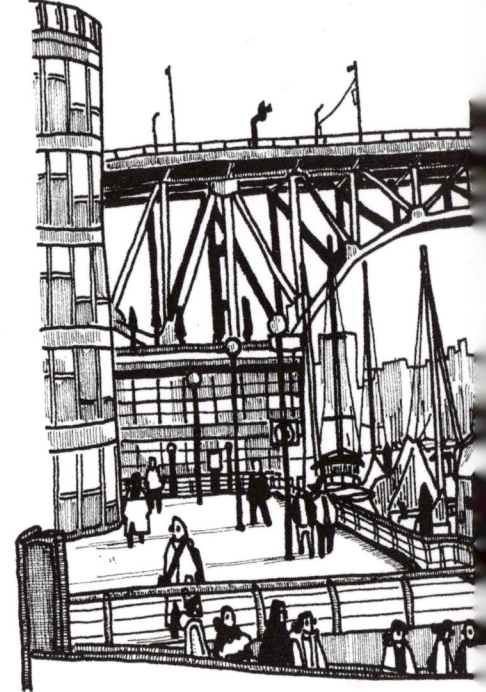

↑ *A drawing with fountain pen (black ink) and acrylic markers— light and dark blue*

## LINES AND COLORS

Carry one trusted pen for linework, and up to two tools for colors. These can be brushes, markers, pencils, or other pens.

## LINES AND MORE LINES

Carry one primary pen to draw with and two fineliners (one thinner and one thicker). Different linewidths are useful when working without color.

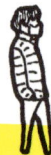

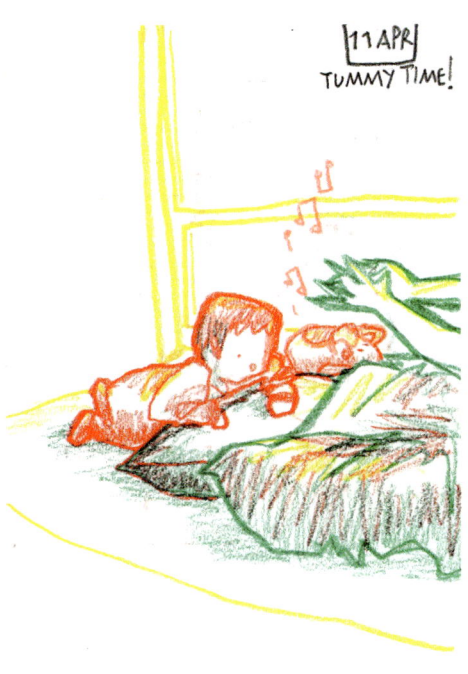

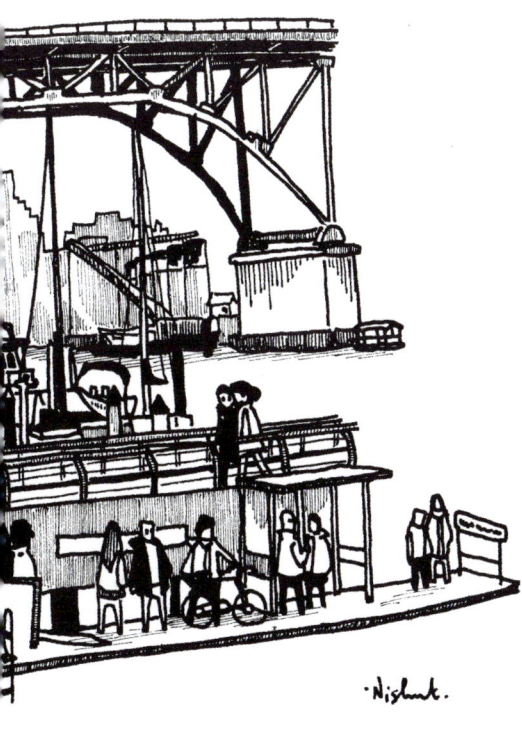

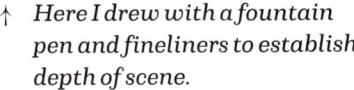

↑ *Here I drew with a fountain pen and fineliners to establish depth of scene.*

↑ *Experimenting with colored pencils while sketching my infant son*

## ONLY THREE COLORS

Take three colors at a time. Think warm, cool, and a bold highlight. Carry a different combination of three every time, keeping in mind colors are not correct or incorrect in isolation—they are relational. A three-color challenge is a good way to learn which colors work best with each other. See the example images: red, yellow, and green to draw my son during tummy time.

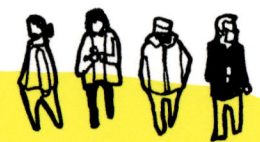

# The Art is Sneaky Too

Earlier in this chapter, I mentioned how sneaky art began with me— the artist—being sneaky. I was self-conscious, and carrying an unnecessary burden of shame. But as I let curiosity light my way, I discovered the joys of being sneaky in the pursuit of art. The more I looked, the more art I could find. Even in the most ordinary places, on the most ordinary days, there was always something interesting.

Sometimes I was motivated by shapes. Sometimes I was excited by human interactions. Sometimes it was the sense of being witness to a special moment that would be lost forever if I did not grab my sketchbook immediately.

But the more I drew, the more I realized it was not always about me being sneaky. The art was sneaky too! That is how I hit upon the second meaning of sneaky art: sneaky art is the beauty of our world, ever-present and hidden in plain sight, waiting to be found. All it needed was my time, the willingness to draw, and the gift of attention. In return, it would make my whole world much more beautiful.

The superpower of making sneaky art is that I am never bored. Any situation can be interesting, and every place has a hidden beauty for me to discover. I am exploring all the time, and finding great rewards from this simple practice.

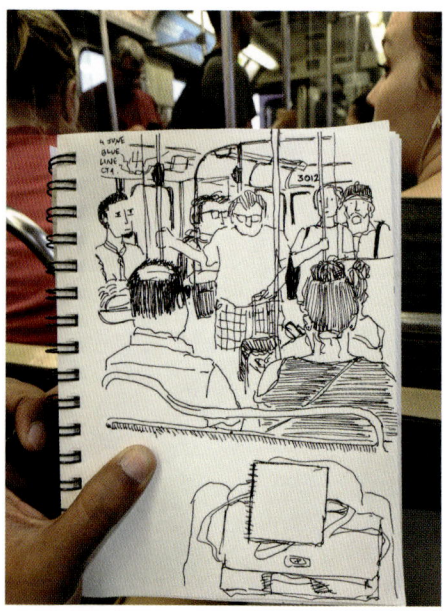

↑ *On the CTA Blue Line in Chicago, I observed how strangers stood beside one another. For a moment, their lives had intersected, but only a moment.*

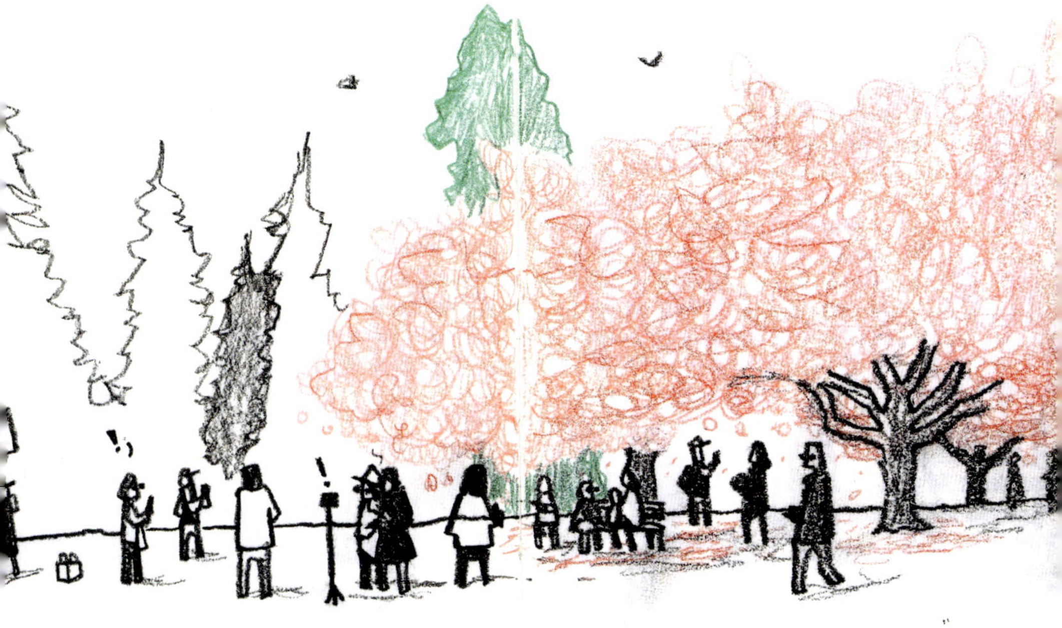

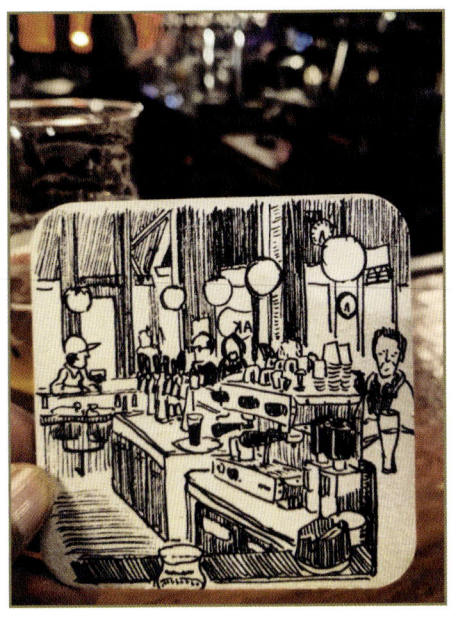

↑ *The park near my home in Vancouver, Canada, is full of blossoming cherry trees every spring. These gorgeous trees attract a lot of social media influencers too!*

← *At a bar in the Netherlands, I started drawing on my coaster while waiting for friends.*

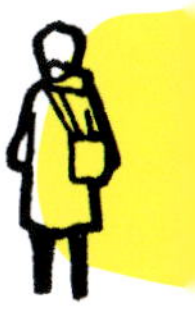

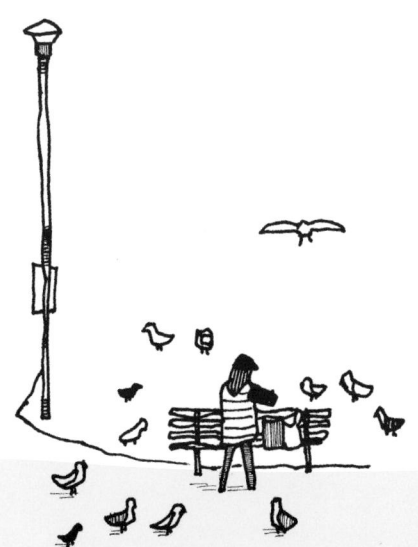

# CHAPTER 2
## BEFORE THE BEGINNING:
## DEFEAT THE BLANK PAGE

# What Is a Blank Page to You?

What do you see when you see a blank page? Does it strike fear in your heart? Does it leave you paralyzed? Do you see an infinite nothingness? Or is it a strange kind of everything-ness?

For the longest time, I was intimidated by the blank page. It was such a pure and perfect thing. I hesitated to ruin it with my bad lines and ugly shapes. Hesitations led to second thoughts. Second thoughts amplified anxiety. And often, I would end up not drawing at all. The blank page would defeat me.

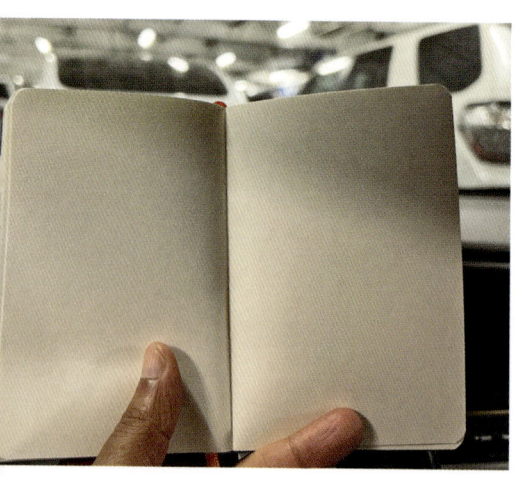

↑ *Parked on the ferry to Vancouver Island*

But to build a drawing habit, we must defeat the blank page. Before hesitations lead to second thoughts and anxiety and reconsiderations, we must strike first! We need a way to stay with that beautiful feeling, that first thought that said it wanted to draw something.

Now, when I buy a new sketchbook, I flip through the pages from back to front. Quickly once, then again more slowly. Of course, the pages are empty. But that is just one way to see. My mind likes to imagine the book as if it is already full, of drawings I will make, of things I will see, of people I will observe. As if the pages already know what they will become one day and forever afterward. As if the pages are simply waiting for me to get started.

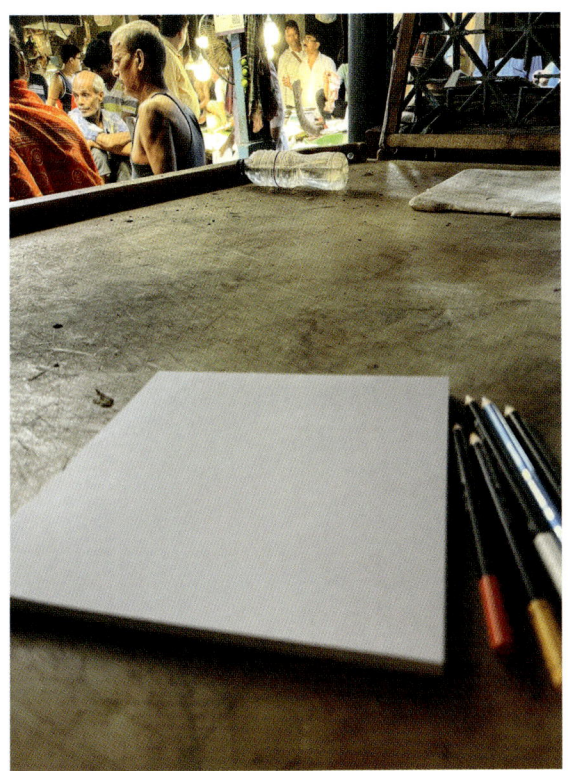

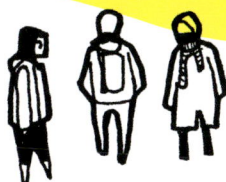

← *In the chaos of Maniktala Fish Market, Kolkata (India)*

It took a long time to see things this way. It took many false starts and nervous first lines. But every blank page is the start of a beautiful journey. And believe it or not, it does not matter how that journey ends. Too many people, before they begin, are obsessed with how things will look at the end, and how others will judge it. But how the drawing looks at the end does not matter. And other people also do not matter.

This book will offer lessons and techniques, but also ideas and thoughts, to help you focus on the journey—this evolving relationship between you and your page. There is great joy in a drawing habit. But finding that joy requires us to stop caring what other people think. It needs us to stop listening even to our worst selves—the voice that discourages us from doing a thing because we may not be good enough.

Take the first step. And breathe in the air. Take the second step. Begin to enjoy the view. Keep drawing. Stay connected to the joy of drawing, and you will have defeated the blank page.

# Exercise:
# Free Your Lines

Drawing is not a talent. While some may be quicker to grasp how it works, it is a skill anyone can learn. I believe it is a skill everyone *should* learn, just like being able to write. Drawing is a way to communicate outside of language. It is a way to say things without needing to say things.

In this exercise, we free the lines inside you, the lines that are already yours, drawn in the way only you would draw them. They are waiting for your confidence, your self-belief, and the sketchbook habit that will reinforce those qualities, to bring them out.

## STEP 1 >

Draw a box. Start from the top-left corner and go clockwise, or from the bottom-right and go counter-clockwise. Draw the box in a single line, without lifting your pen from the page. Let your line waver. Feel the nib press against the page.

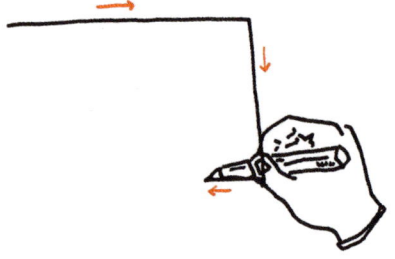

## STEP 2 >

Draw continuous vertical lines inside this box, starting from the middle. Go from top to bottom. Then bottom to top. Then top to bottom again. Keep going, until the box is full of vertical lines.

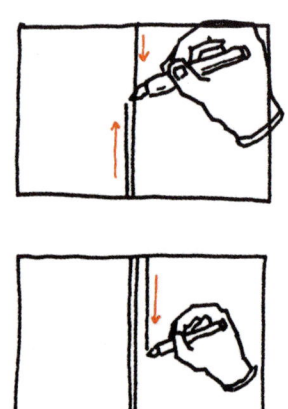

## STEP 3 >

Use the same technique to draw
another box and fill it with
horizontal lines.

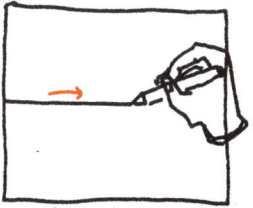

**SNEAKY ART TIP #48**

Your long line contains your thoughts,
your hesitations, your comfort level,
and even your heartbeat. No one can
draw your long line the way you do.
Like your handwriting, it expresses
your unique personality.

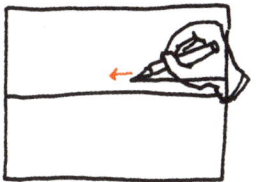

## STEP 4 >

Repeat the steps for a box full of
diagonal lines.

I ask you to draw long, continuous
lines because it is the fastest way to
free your lines. Observe these lines
carefully. They waver, lean, shiver,
deviate, and then subconsciously
correct themselves. They
overcompensate in one direction and
then the other. They move with an
energy that is uniquely yours.

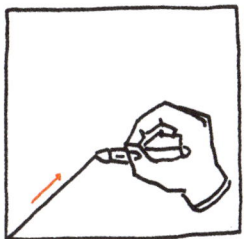

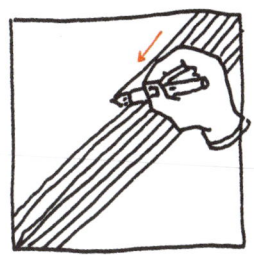

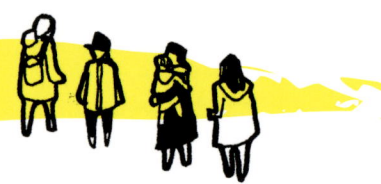

# If You see something, Draw Something

I meet a lot of people who say they do not draw because they are not good at it. My answer is: so what?

What if the practice of drawing is not about being *good at it*? What if the result of your drawing is completely irrelevant? What if drawing is actually just about the process?

Children instinctively know this, but adults are taught to forget. Children draw with pure, *unadulterated* joy. When they are finished, they do not critique or compare their works with others. They toss it behind them and begin a new drawing. Children draw because they find joy in the process of drawing. Adults draw less because life indoctrinates us into an obsession with results. *Is it good enough? Is it worth doing?*

Going out with a sketchbook and pen (or pencil) is a declaration of intent, but not simply to make art (or Art). It is a decision to observe deeply and find something extraordinary in our environments. The act of drawing is much more than the marks made on a page. It is a way to spend the most valuable currency of our lives— our time.

To see something with the intention of drawing it is the act of reducing your complex reality to simple lines, shapes, and colors. It is a way to look past the cynicisms of modern life, without being distracted by our screens, without drowning our thoughts with headphones full of the voices of other people.

A drawing is not about art (or Art). A drawing is about time and attention, and sense and effort. Every mark is the result of a long series of translations and interpretations. What you see at the end, therefore, is so much more than basic ideas of good or bad. It is the output of your various filters, conscious and subconscious, of your body and mind. Drawing is a way to understand your world as you see it and, by extension, a way to understand yourself. Inside and outside.

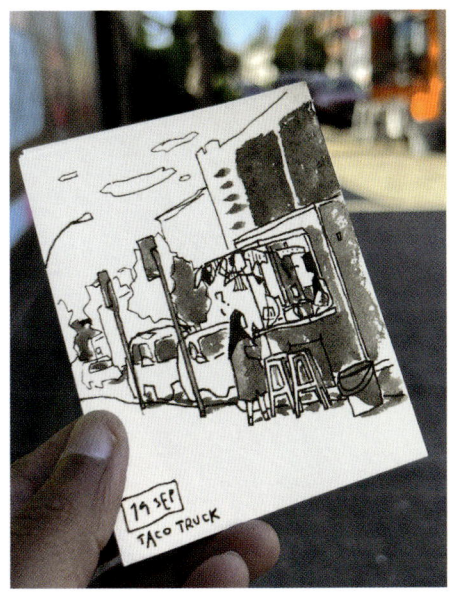

↑ *Waiting for tacos, Vancouver*

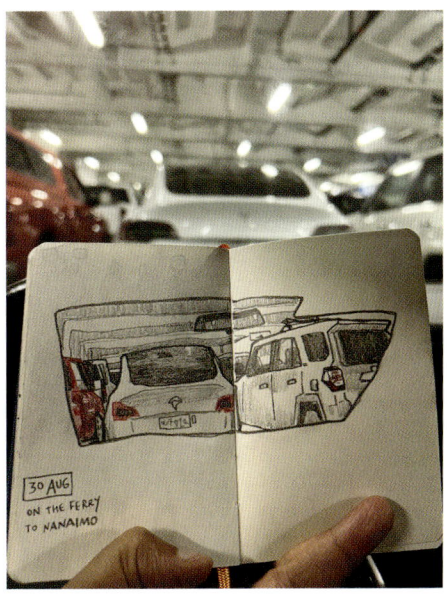

↑ *Windshield as frame and pencil shading to tell light from dark*

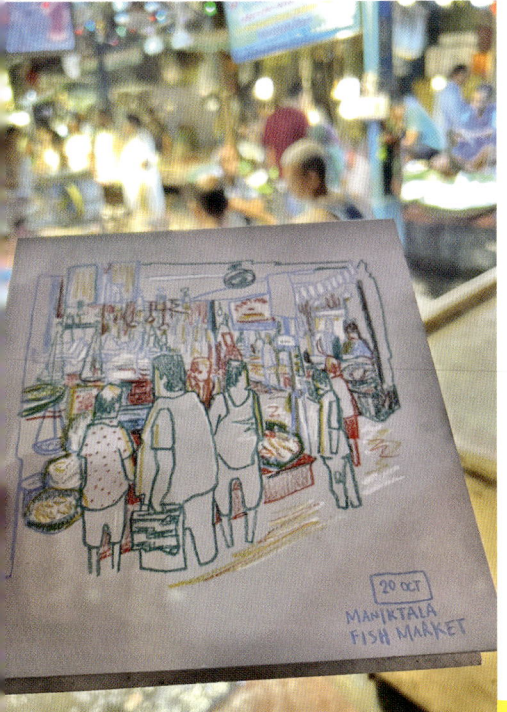

← *Capturing the bustling activity of Maniktala Fish Market in India with colored pencils*

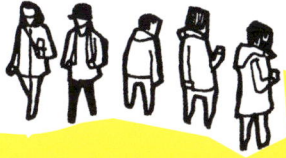

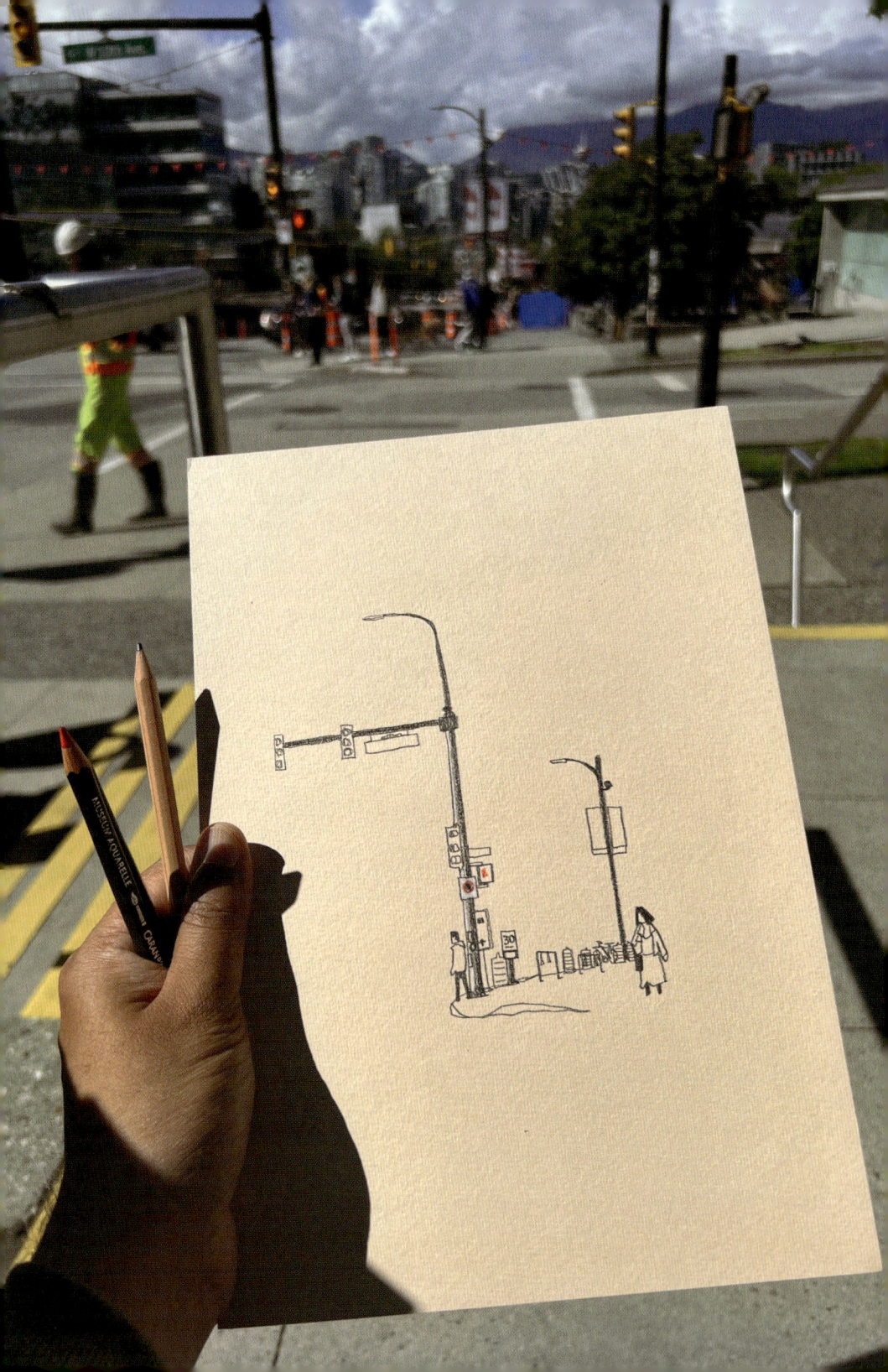

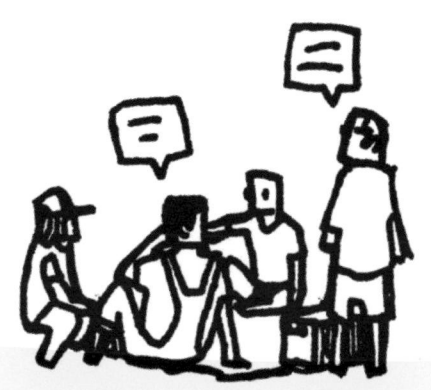

# CHAPTER 3
## FIRST STEPS:
## GET STARTED QUICKLY

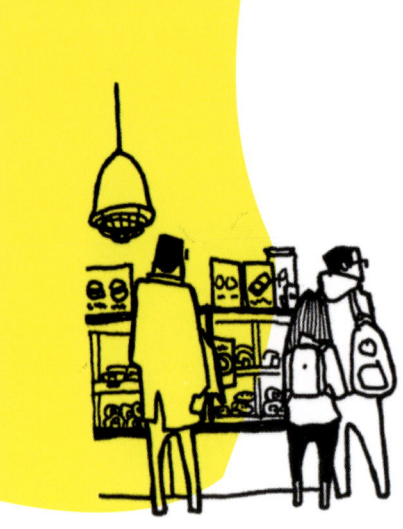

## Keep It Simple

Every drawing you make makes the next one easier. Easier to begin, easier to finish. But often, getting started is much harder than finishing. Many people struggle with incomplete drawings, but far more people struggle against the blank page—because they do not know how to get started, because they are afraid of ruining it, because they think they are not good enough.

When I was afraid of the blank page, when I was afraid of making bad lines, when I thought I was not good enough, there was still one little thing that worked like magic every time. I knew it, and I chased after it: the moment I touched pen to paper, most of my doubts immediately disappeared.

The joy of drawing begins with the first stroke itself.

And it does not take much to get going. It can be just an idea. Like a seed or a clue or curiosity. You may not even be able to put it into words. That's okay. Drawing is a way to indulge that deep, unexplored part of your mind that exists outside of your vocabulary.

Consider this starting point: when you look at your environment, what makes you curious? When I started my sketchbook habit, I was chasing my curiosity for a new city, as well as the people with whom I shared it. Drawing was not only about drawing; it was equally about exploration and discovery.

I explored my outer world and learned to see it in a new light. The artist's eye appreciated café seating that made sneaky art possible, windows that served as frames to look into or out of, traffic lights that halted the cars and pedestrians, and subway stations where humanity congregated. Every page was an exploration of my new world. This outer exploration as an immigrant was matched by a voyage of inner discovery. The more I observed, the more I learned about *myself*—such as my curiosity for human interactions and my love of public spaces.

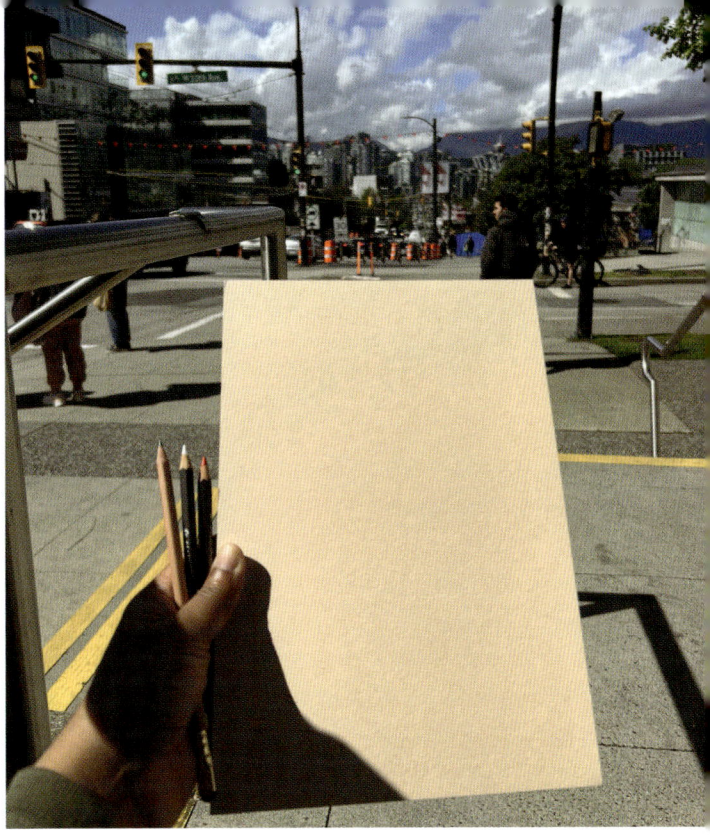

→ *Ready to sketch*

So, what do you find interesting? Maybe you cannot think of something right away. That's all right. Sometimes the act of drawing works as revelation—the effect uncovers the cause. Answers appear line after line, page after page, as the questions flit through your mind. *What caught my eye? Why is this shape interesting? What makes that a good line?*

Trusting your curiosity is not easy. Most of us have internalized harmful ideas of our inadequacy over the years. To begin, we have to let go of the intrusive thoughts that discourage us. We have to make room for ourselves.

I know I have used a lot of words to say this, but it is actually very simple: Allow yourself to look and observe and wait for that signal of curiosity from your brain. Then, begin drawing.

On a sunny afternoon in Vancouver, I watched pedestrians and vehicles under gently floating clouds. I could see people right in front of me, and the mountains far away, and clouds high above. *So close, and so far, inside just one frame*, I thought.

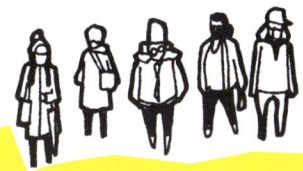

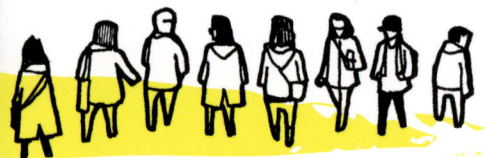

# Build a Curiosity Spiral

What is the first thing that catches your eye? There are no wrong answers. Anything will do. It could be a person. Or a tree. A building. Or a stop sign.

This first point of interest will be the center of your curiosity spiral. As you spiral away from the point, you move away from what you found interesting. The farther you drift, the less curious you become. The less curious you become, the less attention you give to those parts of the page, to those parts of your scene. Less attention equals less time equals fewer lines and fewer details.

Your curiosity spiral is unique to you. It shows you what you like and how much. It tells you what you do not care for. (Psst, I don't care for long lines of windows and architectural details on buildings.)

Your curiosity spiral serves two important functions:

> **For the viewer:** An outward spiral of curiosity is also an inward spiral of information. The human eye follows the flow of information, and with a carefully planned spiral, you can subconsciously motivate the viewer to follow the path to your initial curiosity.

> **For the artist:** This technique will save you a lot of time and energy. By starting at your point of curiosity, you start with joy and discovery. By allowing yourself to follow the spiral, you let yourself spend less time, energy, and attention on parts that do not interest you. You do not have to give equal attention to every part of your scene! Knowing this will make many busy, complicated scenes less intimidating.

A curiosity spiral will make it easier to get started. As we will see in upcoming exercises, even five minutes is long enough to start *and* finish a sketch!

→ *Under a warm sun in Vancouver, I was struck by the sight of a person standing under the tall traffic light, waiting for permission to cross.* City life, *I thought*, runs on many such unspoken agreements. The cars have their turn to go, just like the pedestrians do.

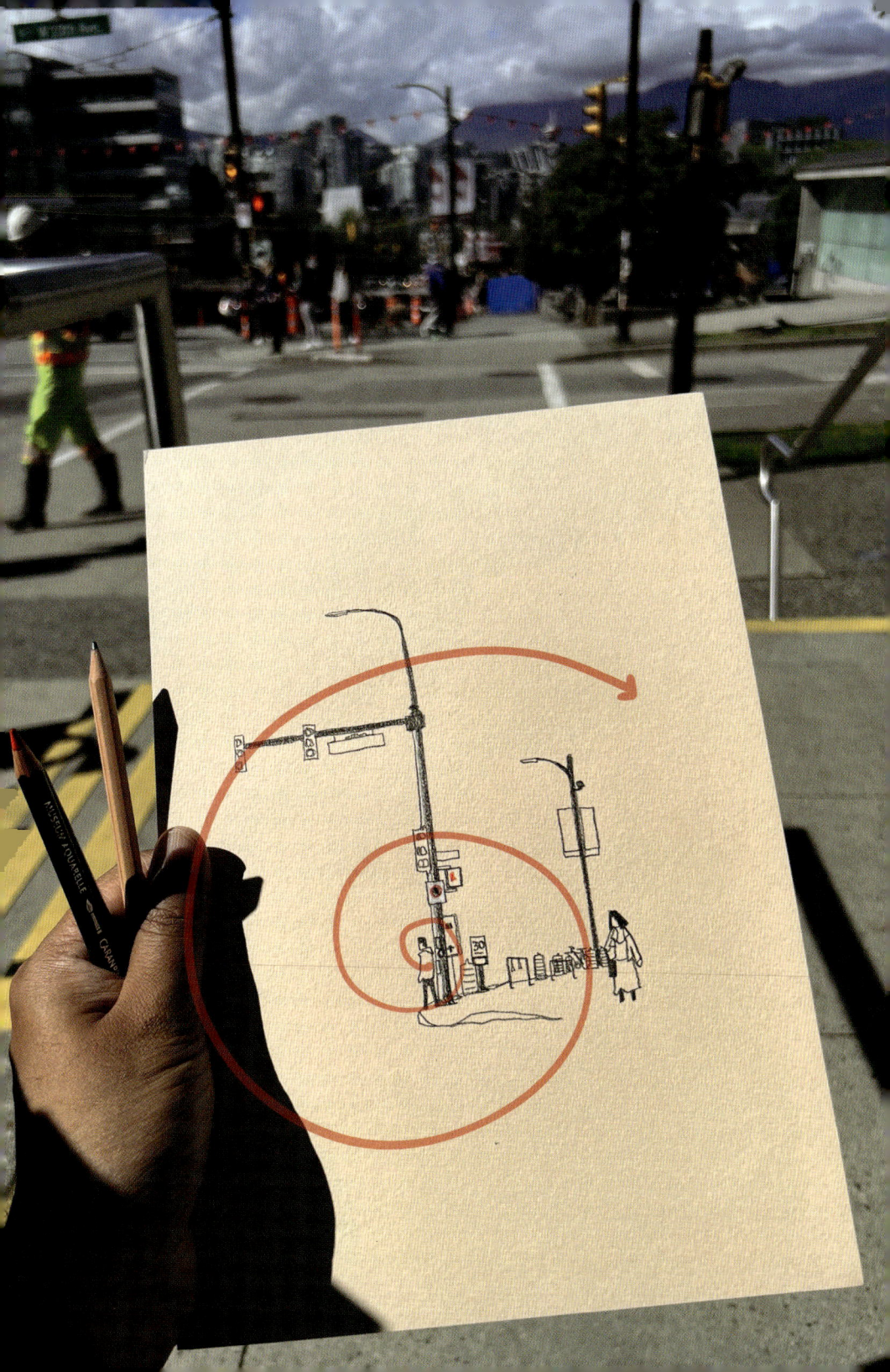

# Mapping and Using Anchors to Find Your Way

You may worry about how everything will fit. You may worry about getting the proportions right. These are legitimate concerns. But remember, by starting at a point of interest and spiraling out, by starting quickly without planning the entire page, you commit to going step by step, object by object, steadily moving forward.

A simple trick to keep in mind is that everything you draw must help you draw the next thing. After drawing one object, I look for where I can jump from it. What sits beside it? What looms over or lies under it? What is juxtaposed next to it?

The map of your page constructs itself based on how much time, attention, and space you gave to the first thing you drew—which was hopefully the most interesting thing to you.

Anchors help you jump from one object to the next. They also give you a sense of scale for the next object, and the one after that, and the one after that.

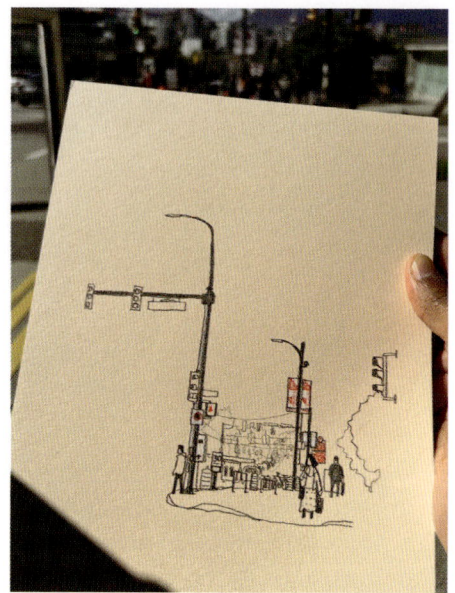

↑ *The traffic light pole helped me scale the rest of the middle ground and background. From its base I drew the sidewalk. Referencing the signs on it, I knew how tall my people needed to be. Looking into the horizon, it also told me how high the mountains would stand, and the cars and the poles farther down the road.*

# Layers! Layers! Layers!

A drawing is a translation of a three-dimensional environment onto a two-dimensional page. In other words, a drawing is a *flattening* of reality. To create the illusion of depth, our page needs clear and distinct layers.

You can use as many layers as you like, but it is simple to keep a foreground, middle, and background. When you look at what you want to draw, do you see the three layers of your scene? Which layer does your object of interest occupy?

We will give each layer a unique role on the page. Together, they will bring focus to your drawing, give your subject a place of importance, and provide key information or context about the scene itself. For ease of understanding, I call them the Subject Layer, the Frame Layer, and the Extras Layer.

| Layer | Role |
|---|---|
| Subject | Where your point of curiosity lives |
| Frame | Frames or contains your Subject |
| Extras | Gives context and additional info |

Seeing (and drawing) in layers is good for you for the following reasons:

> It helps you save time when drawing on location. By giving each layer its own role, it becomes easier to take on complicated and busy cityscapes. Each layer does not need the same amount of time and attention.

> Layering helps you focus on what you care about. By relegating the extra elements to the Extras layer, you focus on the joy of drawing instead of getting tangled in tedious lines. At the same time, you also help your viewer see where your attention lies, i.e., where *their* attention should be too.

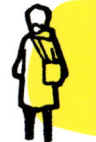

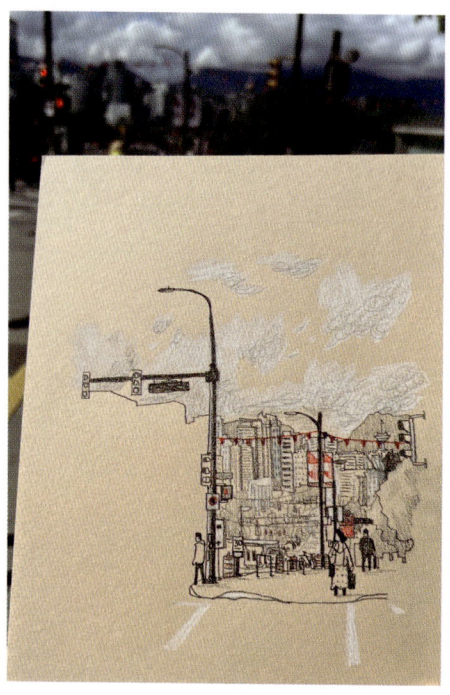

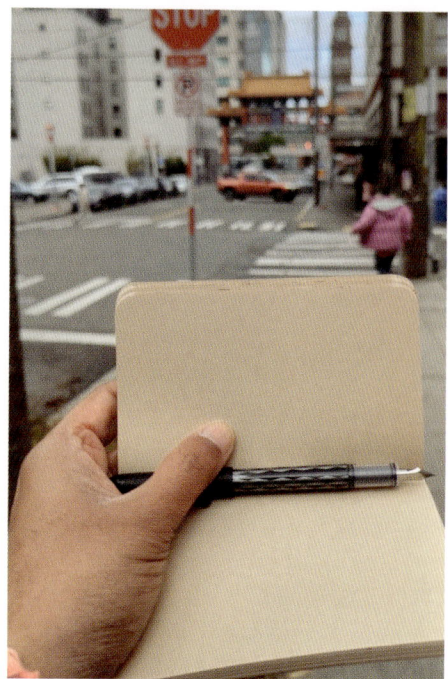

↑ *Under the warm sun of Vancouver, my subjects are the people waiting to cross the street in the foreground. The frame is in the middle ground—from the outline of the building on the left, and the second lamppost and red streamers, to the edge of the trees on the right side. The background layer provides essential information about the location and time of year: it is a beautiful summer sky, and you can see all the way past the skyscrapers of downtown Vancouver to the mountains on the northern horizon.*

↑ *On a cold morning in Seattle's Chinatown, I thought about heritage buildings and modern architecture, and how both must live and grow together in big cities. My interest was sparked by a stop sign. From my perspective, it appeared larger than the entrance gate to Chinatown. It was as big as the church spire in the distance. It was bright red against a gray sky. By drawing the stop sign first, I could measure everything else on the page against it. It became my scale for the rest of the scene.*

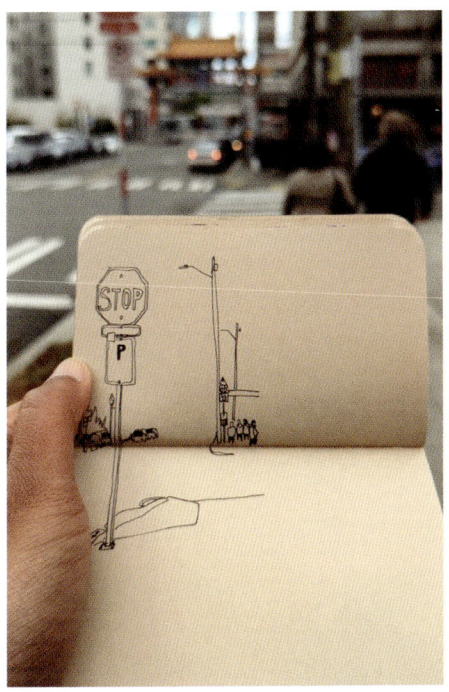

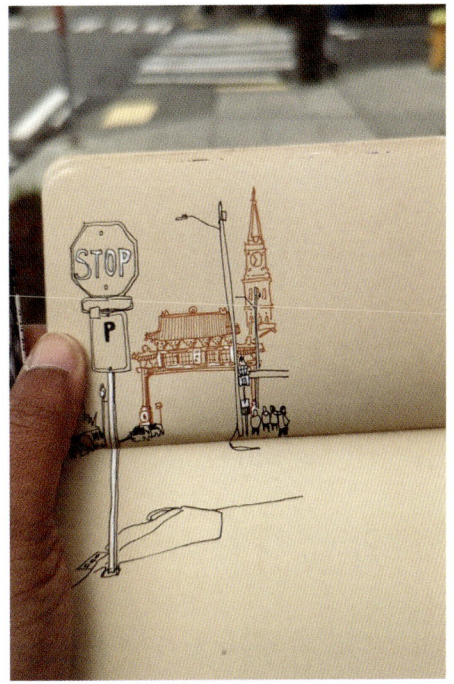

↑ *The stop sign gave me starting points for the building right behind it, the entrance to Chinatown, the lamppost across the street, and the street intersection itself. The stop sign became what I like to call an "anchor" for the other objects.*

↑ *My object of interest (the stop sign) is in the foreground. That becomes the Subject Layer. In the middle ground are two lampposts and the edges of two buildings. My subject sits between them, as if framed by them. This makes the middle ground my Frame Layer. The background becomes the Extras layer, providing essential information about this part of the city (the Chinatown entrance) and my point of view. By using another color for the background layer, I emphasize that it is an extra layer, not a part of the main composition.*

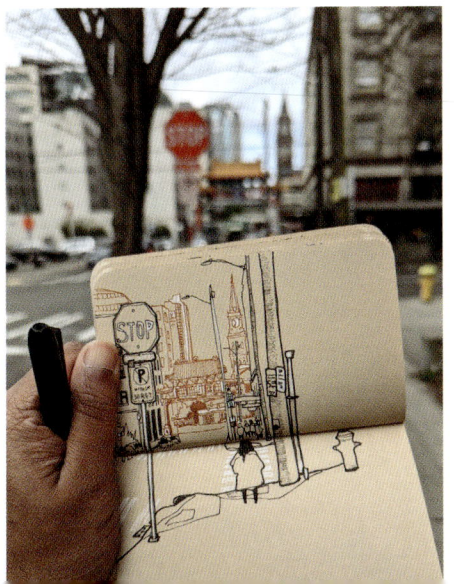

← *The finished sketch*

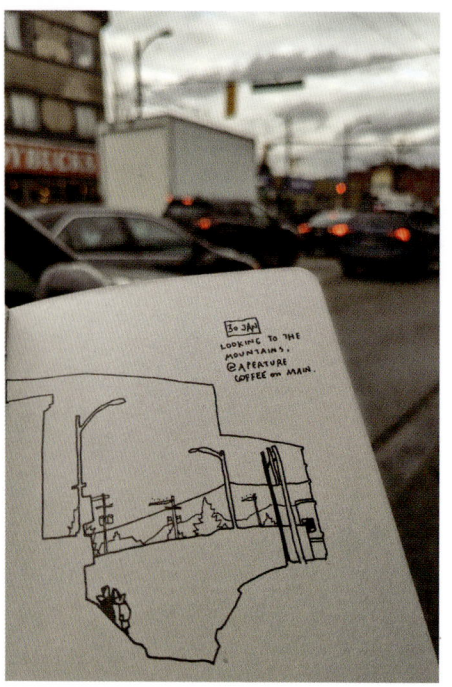

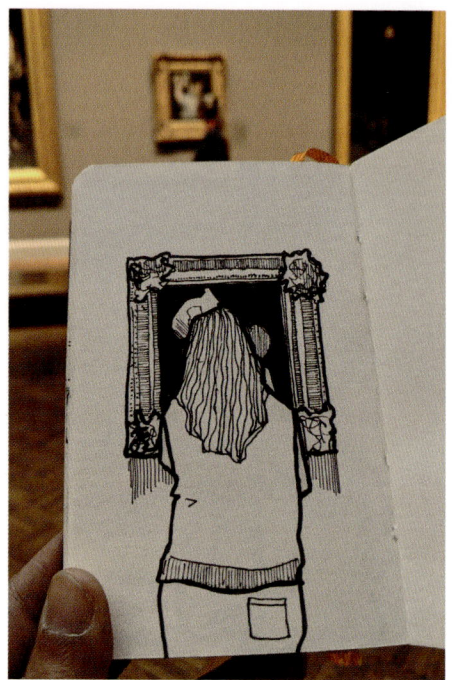

## SOME LAYERING EXAMPLES

Layering has helped me get started on challenging scenes, because I know I do not have to worry about what I do not care for. Here are some quick sketches, often drawn standing up, usually within a sharp time limit.

↑ *On an overcast afternoon in Vancouver, the foreground is a frame through which we see the scene. The two human subjects are in the middle. Behind them, the background depicts the setting of this scene.*

**F: Frame**
**M: Subject**
**B: Extra**

↑ *At the Art Institute of Chicago, a person standing in front of a rich frame of fine art became the subject in the foreground. The frame itself becomes their frame, in the background. In this scene there is no middle layer.*

**F: Subject**
**M: N/A**
**B: Frame**

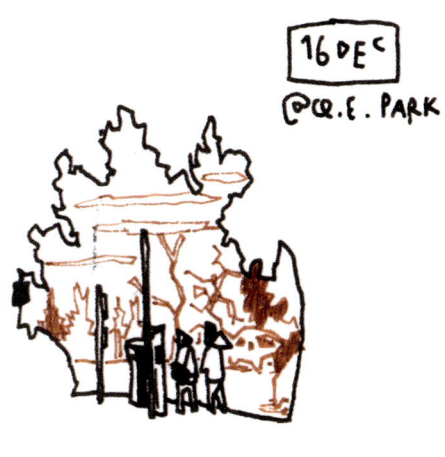

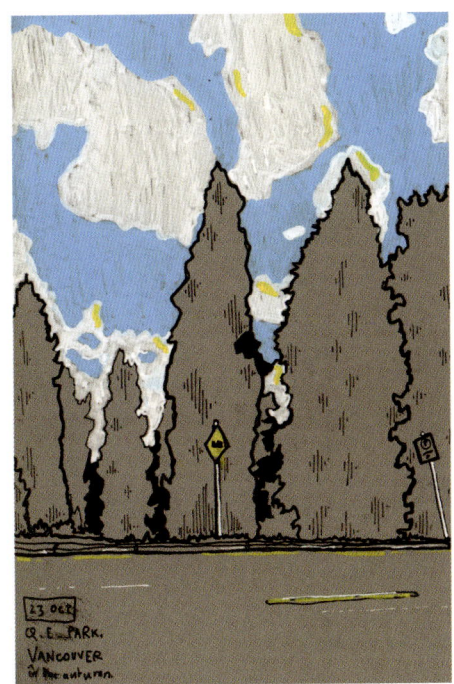

↑ In the park near my home, two people and the parking meter became my subjects in the foreground. The canopy of trees around them is a middle-ground frame. Looking through this frame, the background is the extras layer, giving information about the setting.

**F: Subject**
**M: Frame**
**B: Extra**

↑ What is the subject of this page? Sometimes I think it is the trees, but sometimes I think the clouds are the subject. The foreground is an extras layer, depicting only the street and street sign. In the middle are the trees, whose profiles act as a frame upon which sits the background, a bright blue sky with playful clouds.

**F: Extras**
**M: Frame**
**B: Subject**

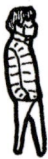

# Quick Drawing Challenges

Opportunities to draw can strike suddenly. We must be ready to tackle them. Here are some ideas on how to do so:

## LOOK FOR NATURAL FRAMES

Natural frames are elements in your environment that work like frames! Inside them, or around them, or because of them, your attention is drawn toward something interesting.

How would the drawing change if your subject was in front of the frame instead of behind it?

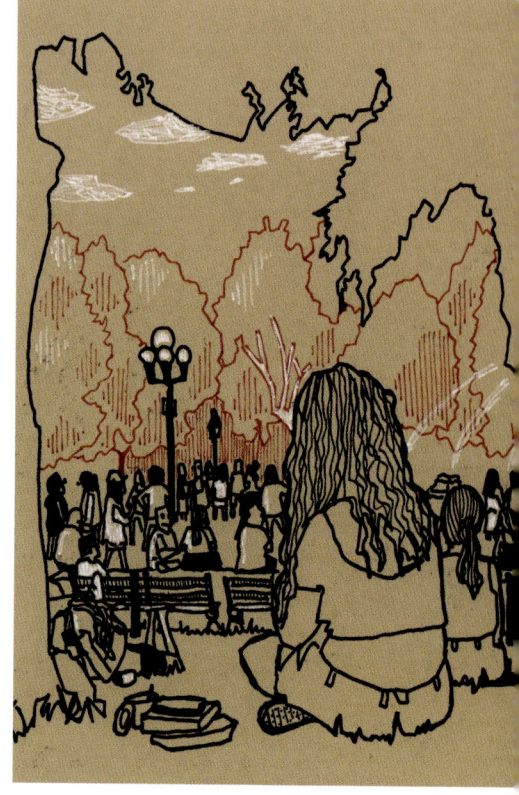

↑ *On a warm day in Washington Square Park in New York, my frame begins at the left foreground and travels to the right middle ground, enclosing my subject (seated, in the foreground).*

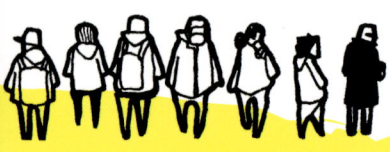

## FILTER IN, FILTER OUT

When looking at a densely packed scene, zoom in to focus only on a part of it. Does the drawing become simpler? Does it bring better attention to your subject if you filter out the "unnecessary bits?"

## CONTRASTS

Sometimes one element is interesting only when contrasted against another element. Elements in your scene are in conversation with each other. You get to decide which conversation to highlight. This is a creative decision that elevates your scene beyond mere drawing skill.

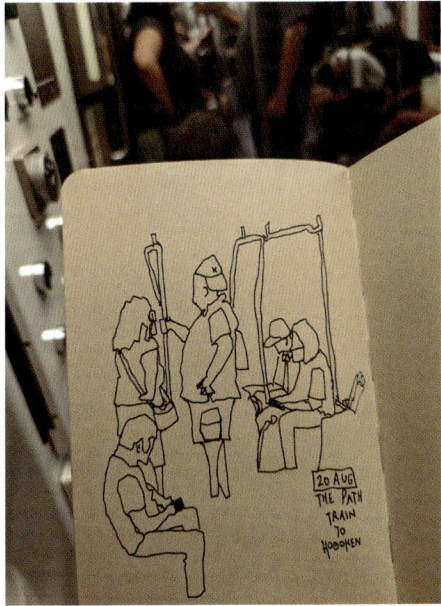

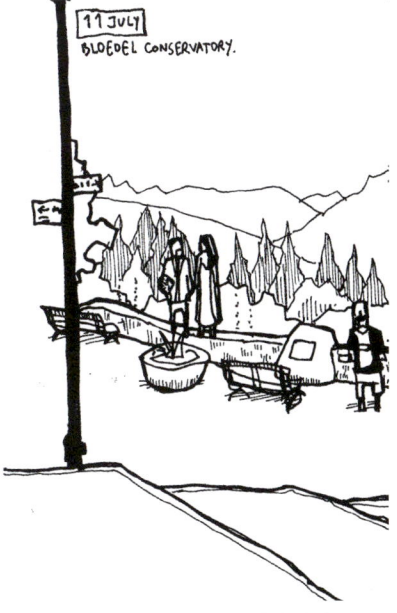

↑ On the NYC subway, I drew only the people and the poles they hung on to. I did not have time to pay attention to the rest of the scene, and it also felt unnecessary to what I wanted to show.

↑ Observe here the contrast between two human activities at the same spot—a tourist and a wedding photoshoot—both drawn to the same location for similar reasons.

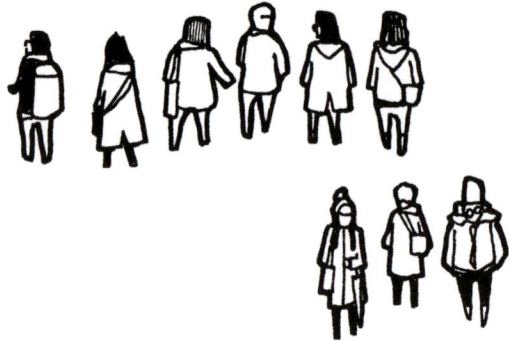

## PLAY WITH COLORS

Colors on your page do not have
to depict realism. Can you use one
color for your subject of interest and
another for everything else? Does
this help your subject become more
prominent? Does it help a viewer
focus? Just as important, does it make
it easier to finish the drawing in time?

→  *In the park near my home, I used a*
   *different color for the background*
   *to set it apart from my subject: the*
   *person in the foreground looking at*
   *the plants.*

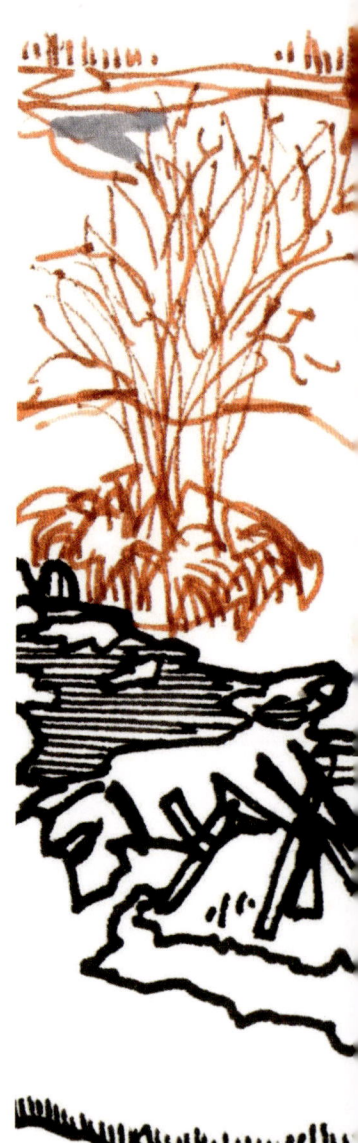

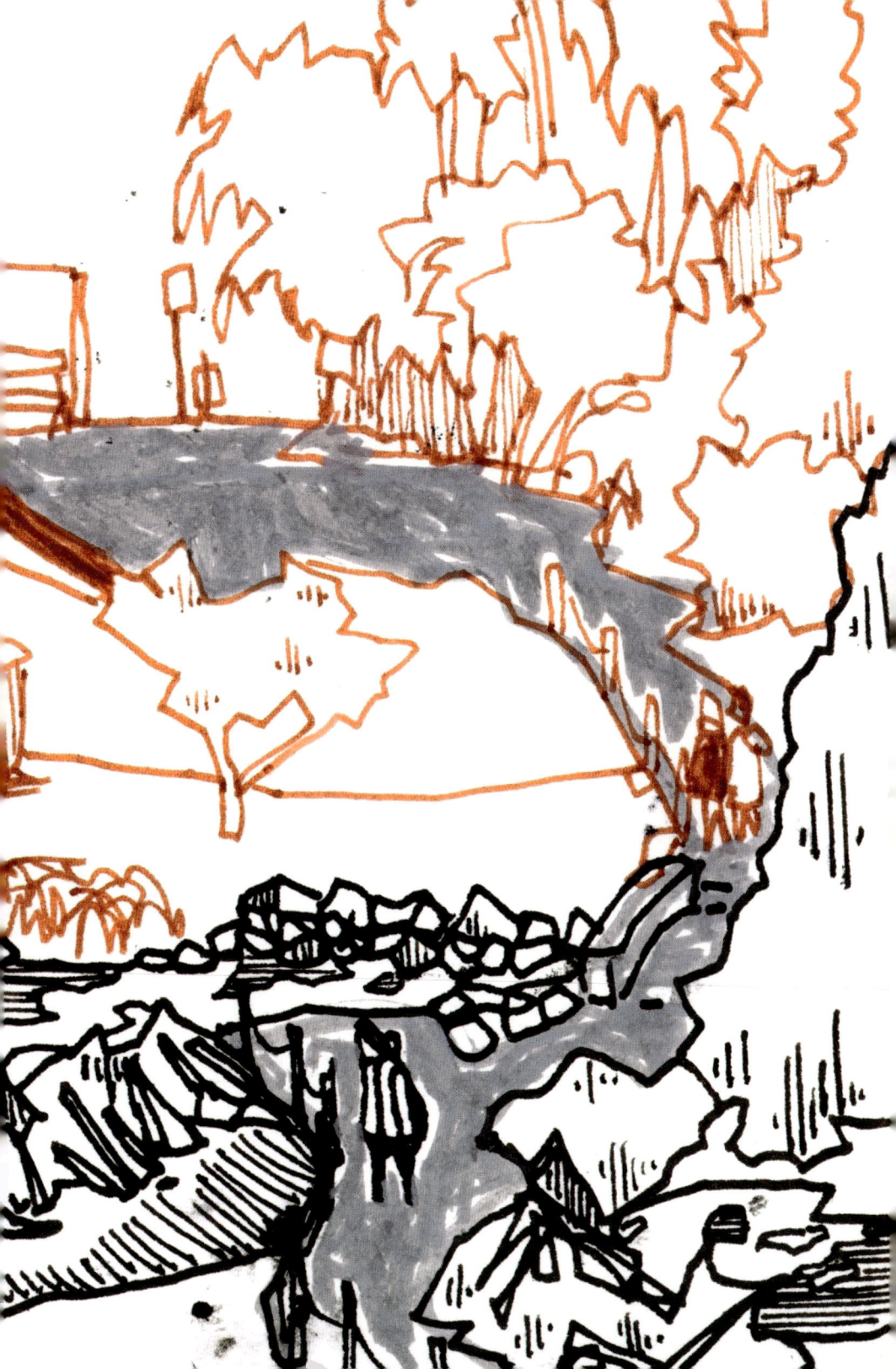

→ *Drawing to live music allows your art to resonate with another art. Note how the lines move. Do they dance? Note how you move. Are you tapping your foot?*

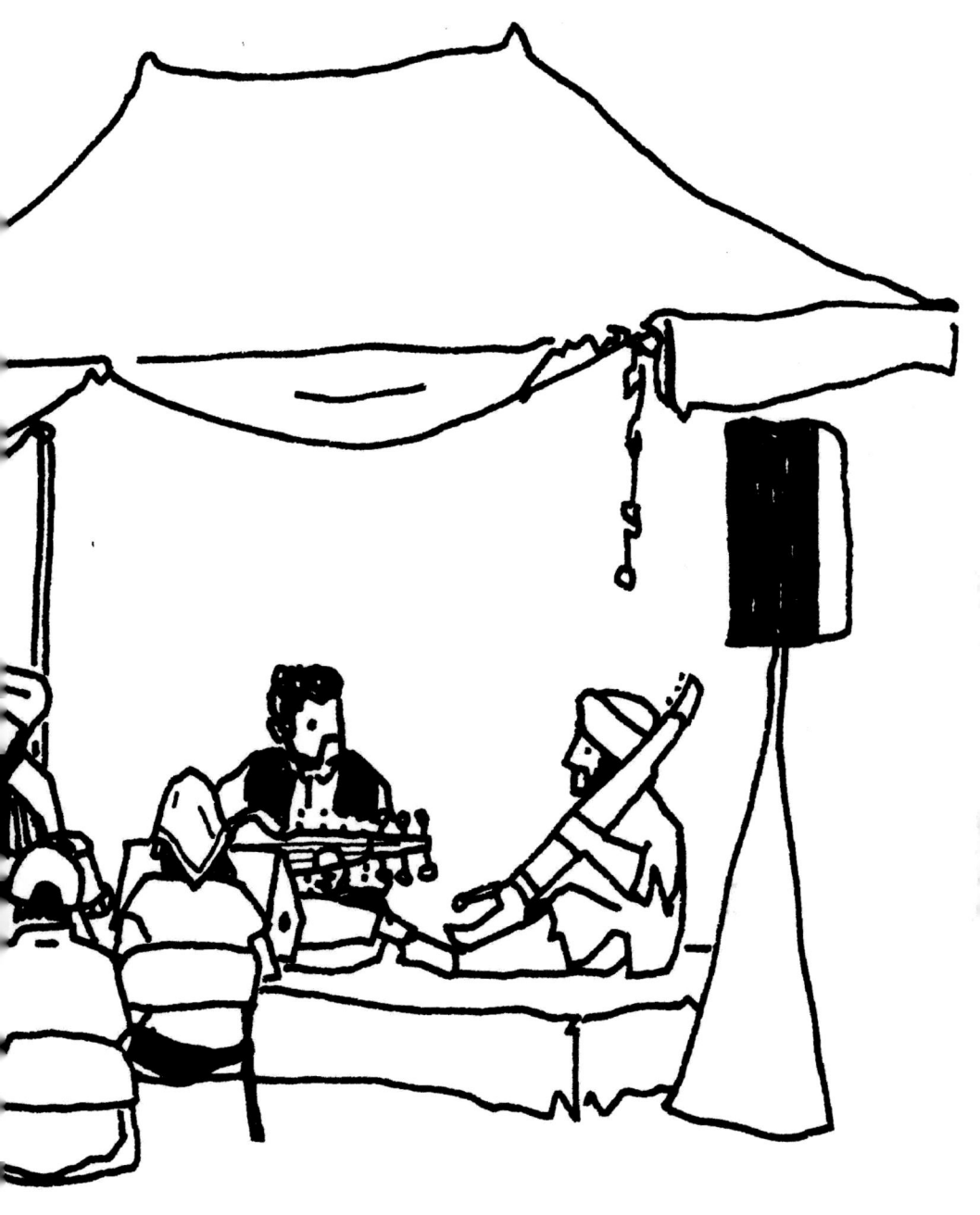

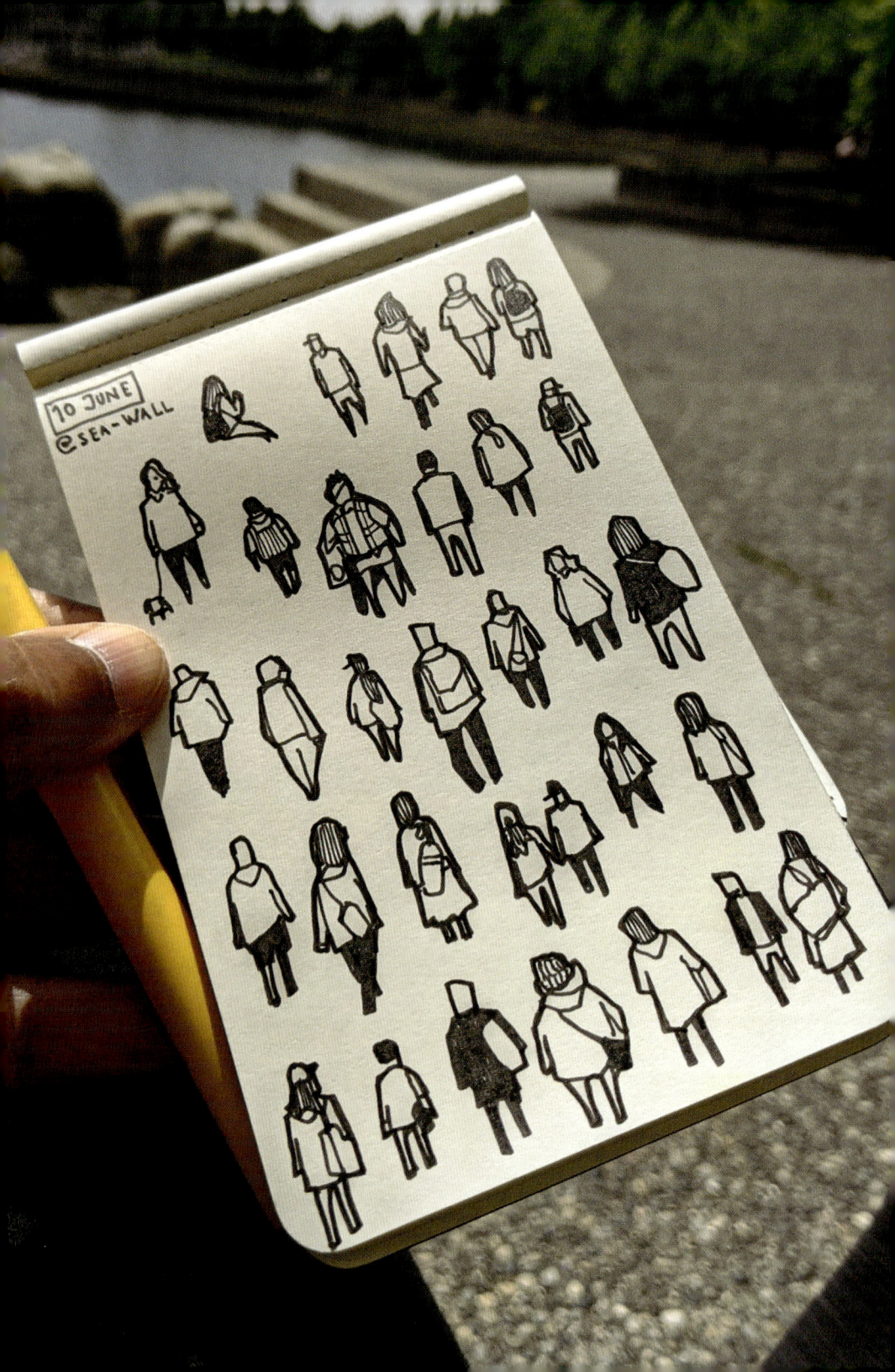

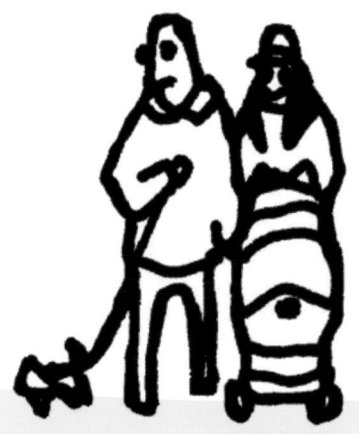

# CHAPTER 4
## GOOD IDEAS:
## ON THE PATH TO STYLE

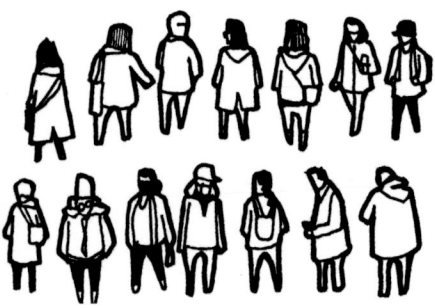

# How Do You Find Your Style?

For the longest time, I thought *style* was a mysterious virtue possessed only by talented people. For the longest time, I believed that *talent* was something you were born with, something impossible to acquire later in life. So when I struggled to improve or discover a style, I believed it was because I was not talented. It took several years, and hundreds of sketchbook pages, to understand how wrong I was about all of it.

This is the most frequently asked question whenever people see my work: "How did you find your style?"

They ask because, like younger me, they are looking for clues about where to go and what to do. They want to know if it was a little trick they missed somehow, a simple thing that would unlock their best work.

Sometimes they say, "I wish I was talented, like you."

And I know the word means to them what it meant to me once upon a time. People say it as a compliment, but it is a loaded word fraught with uncomfortable, inaccurate interpretations. It makes the claim that the journey was easier for me. *It was not.* It suggests that I always had direction and purpose. *I did not.* It implies that they would do it too, if they were similarly blessed.

This common notion of talent harms both parties. It neglects my years of struggle through self-doubt, and the difficult journey that often felt like stumbling in the dark. It diminishes my resolve and determination to keep going. But besides myself, it also dampens the energy and enthusiasm with which everyone should approach their art practice.

In my experience many people who use the word "talent" for others disqualify themselves from this enriching and fruitful creative pursuit because they consider themselves not talented. There is an implication that an art practice is not worth the effort if our work does not look as good as someone else's. Talent reduces the value of the struggle, the hardships of the journey, by suggesting that creative work should be done only when it comes easily to us. But struggling is not an indication of failure, or a signal to give up.

The path to style is full of self-doubts and failures. Without them, you would not know which way to push. You have to keep pushing. You have to try something and fail. Try again and fail again. You have to follow various inspirations even in the face of failures. Failing, failing, failing, again and again. You have to enjoy the failures because they are an essential part of your journey.

In this chapter, I want to show you how a journey full of failures is a beautiful thing. This chapter consists of thoughts and ideas to help you enjoy every moment of your creative journey. But I also know how difficult that can be these days.

We are under the relentless assault of perfect images made by perfect artists working out of perfect studios surrounded by perfect vibes. Our devices throw images at us from all over the world that both inspire and intimidate us. How did *they* find their style? Social media has implanted the false idea that we should be finished products and polished brands and fully formed creatives. But no artist is ever done *becoming*. We are all works-in-progress. We are all on our various journeys. The point of your journey is not for it to be finished, or for you to become a finished product. Art is an infinite game.

You have to love playing the game. Because what is style anyway? Is it a difficult thing done effortlessly? Is it a trick no one knows but you? Is it a vision that only you have? In this chapter I want to unpack the idea of style and show how its pieces are already inside you. You only have to put them together in a way that works. These pieces are your personality, your likes and dislikes, your joys and frustrations, and your idiosyncrasies. Your confidence is important, but self-doubt also plays a vital role. Your lopsided skills matter, just like your poorly absorbed ideas.

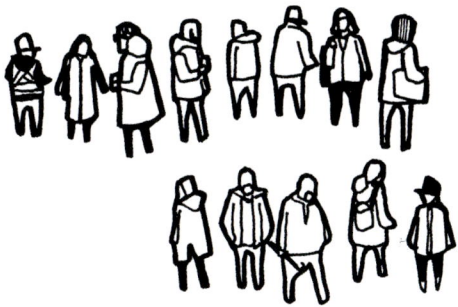

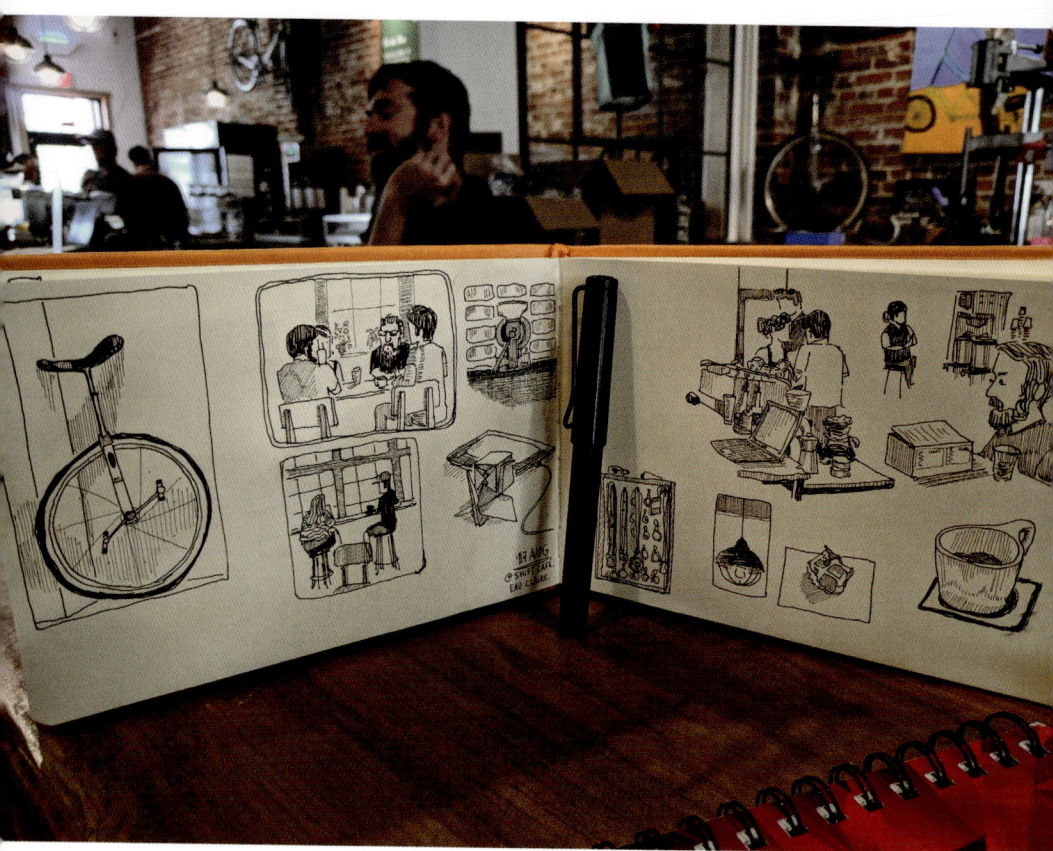

Your style is nothing more than the most authentic representation of you on the page. It takes honesty for style to emerge, and the confidence to be honest. It takes vulnerability, which is the courage you need to face the blank page.

It also takes time to access these qualities and express them. Because, most importantly, doing so requires you to get out of your own way. In the following pages, I share important ideas that will help you get out of your own way.

↑ *Getting comfortable at the local café, Eau Claire, Wisconsin*

The further you go, the more joy you will find. The happier you are, the easier it will be to put yourself on the page. And one day others will look at your work and say you have a style. *How did you find it?* they will ask.

# Trusting Your Instincts

Most people have a sense of what they like, even if they cannot say why. But instead of trusting their instincts, they doubt themselves and devalue their curiosity.

Curiosity is key. It is the beautiful human trait that needs to be nurtured and cultivated. If you allow it, every page of your sketchbook can be a lesson in cultivating curiosity and trusting your instincts.

The best way I know to begin trusting your instincts is a practice of quick sketching. Set yourself a five-minute daily sketching goal—no more, no less—to go from start to finish. Start quickly, because there is not enough time to hesitate, and finish at the five-minute mark. At this stage, you are not in the business of making good drawings. At this stage, you are subconsciously imbibing the following important lessons:

### TO SEE QUICKLY

Wherever you are, whatever you see, you should be quick to know what you find interesting. A quick sketching habit trains you to notice what catches your eye: color or shapes or lines or compositions.

### TO KILL HESITATIONS

Hesitations do not help at all. Their only job is to stop you from drawing. A five-minute drawing is just a five-minute drawing! A quick sketching habit teaches us to kill our hesitations by lowering the premium to getting started.

### TO GET TO THE END

There is a dopamine rush waiting for you at the end of every sketch. Finishing a sketch is a rewarding feeling. You saw something, you overcame self-doubt, and you finished. You won, and it only took you five minutes!

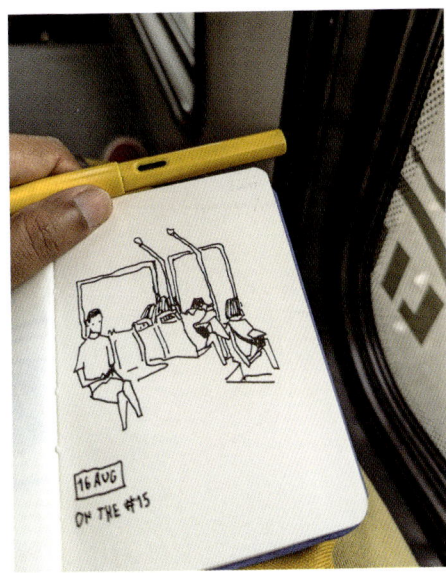

↑  *A quick sketch on the bus*

# Accuracy vs. Precision

As an engineering student, when I learned about control systems, I understood the subtle but significant difference between accuracy and precision. Can you tell?

Accuracy is how exactly correct you are. Did you hit the bull's-eye? When you draw, are your lines *exactly correct? How exactly correct* are the contours of a person's face, or the effect of light and shadow inside a room, or the colors of a lush garden? A high-accuracy drawing would be a hyperrealistic portrait or landscape indistinguishable from a photograph. When we begin to draw, we first strive for accuracy, to try to get everything exactly right.

Precision is not how correct but how consistent you are. Do

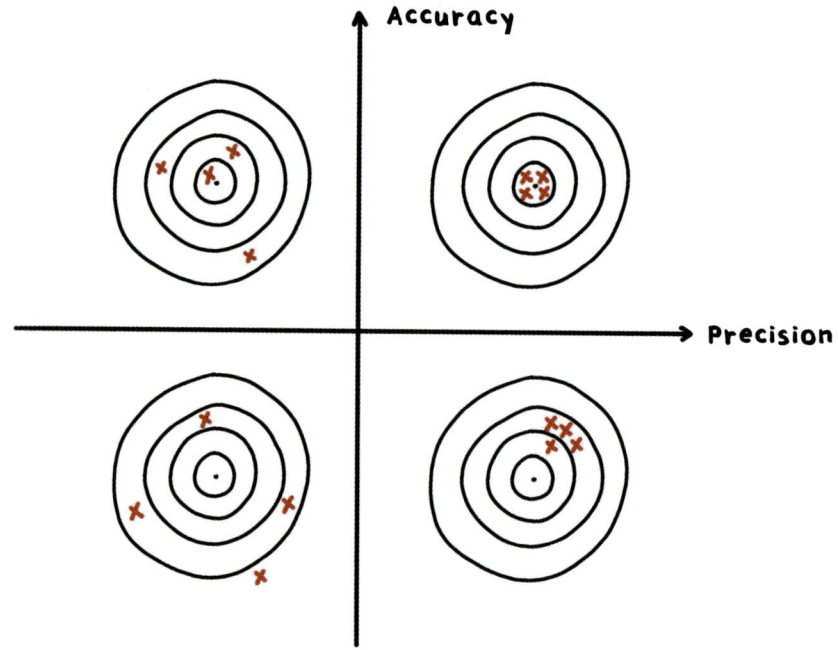

you always draw faces like that? Is your perspective always skewed the same way? Do your lines tilt to the left or right every time? Is the head always too big compared to the body? Consistency is about what you get right but also what you get wrong *the same way, every time.*

Many people believe the job is to be highly accurate. Sometimes they succeed; often they do not. Aiming for high accuracy, they fall into the "high accuracy/low precision" box. Because it is hard!

But not only is it very difficult to be both highly accurate and precise, I think it is also not even necessary. I believe the job of the artist is to be precise. Mistakes are not only unavoidable, but they also are a necessary part of getting to what becomes your style. Because mistakes are not just imperfections. Mistakes are human. And your mistakes are your humanity. Your mistakes are your unique signature on the page.

In workshops, I like to share this quote by my favorite musician, Miles Davis:

"Once is a mistake. Twice, is an idea. Three times is style."

Don't give up on mistakes! Stick with your mistakes to get good ideas. Stay with those ideas, page after page, and they will give you clues. Those clues will develop into your style. Your style is the most authentic representation of you on the page, and your imperfections are part of who you are.

So be very careful with that eraser, or you might accidentally erase yourself from the page!

# Writing and Drawing Are the Same Thing

If you know how to write by hand, you already know how to draw.

In writing, you combine lines to make shapes (letters of the alphabet). You combine those shapes in different ways (words) to describe your world and express yourself (sentences and paragraphs). In drawing, too, you use lines and combinations of lines to make shapes. You combine those shapes in different ways to describe your world and express yourself.

The difference between writing and drawing is a matter of how you put together those lines and shapes. But the important thing to remember is this: just as you have a distinct handwriting, your drawing also already has distinct lines and distinct shapes. You already possess the building blocks of your style. So instead of erasing them, lean into them!

In the next chapter, we will use this idea to draw people.

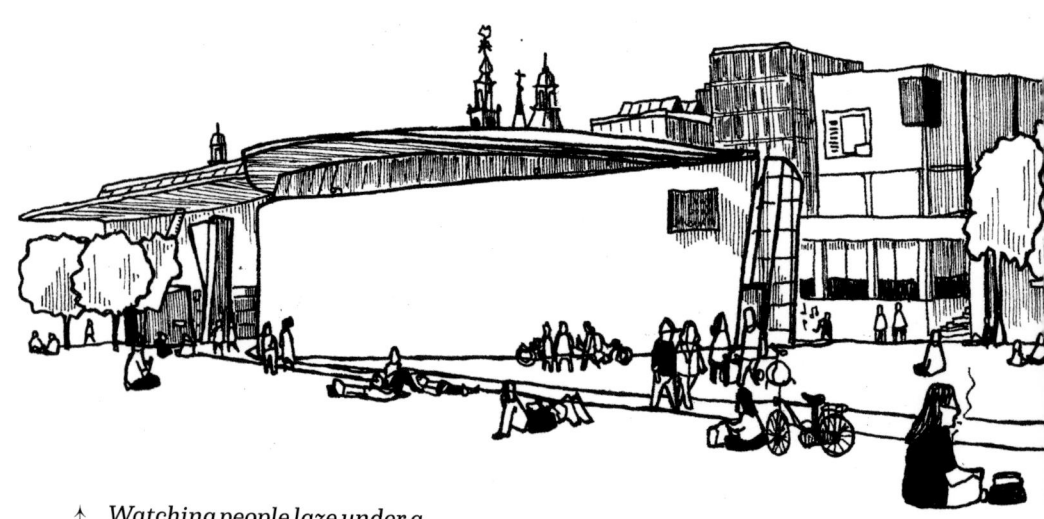

↑ *Watching people laze under a summer sun, I was lazy too. Can you see the long but simple lines and shapes that make up this scene?*

# Exercise:
## Learning to See

Use a sketchbook or the camera on your phone. This exercise is not about drawing per se. It is about what happens before. To know what you should draw, you have to get good at seeing. To get good at seeing, you need to appreciate the filters behind what you see.

Biologically speaking, your eyes have rods and cones to filter light and color, respectively. Based on how well your eyes work, you perceive the lights and shadows of your world, and recognize various colors. But that is not all that seeing is about.

What we really see is what we notice. After the eyes themselves, come the filters of your taste and attention. What do you see, then see again? Where do your eyes linger? What do you recall, and what do you forget even just a few seconds later?

These questions are not meant to be answered, but think of them as prompts for this exercise. Use your sketchbook or camera to start capturing what you notice. Follow instinct. Chase curiosity. Afterward, use these images to spark a conversation with yourself. What can you now tell about what you

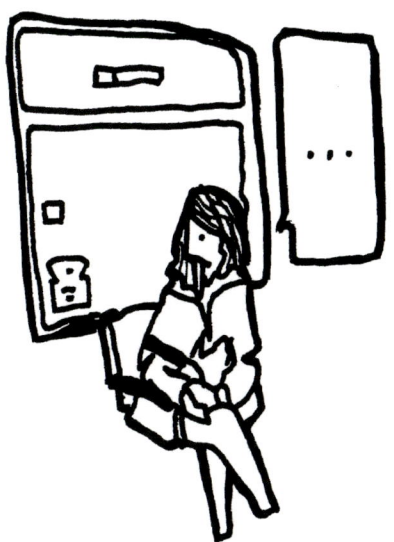

↑ *Seeing someone look out the bus window, I wondered about the complexity of their life and the depth of their thoughts.*

saw, where you lingered, what you remembered, and what grabbed your attention?

Thinking about what you notice will help you see better. Whenever you enter a room, whenever you see a new landscape, within seconds you will have a sense of what you like—colors, lines, shapes, and themes.

There will be ideas in your mind that cannot be put into words. Entire conversations outside of language. They will inform your style in unspoken, subconscious, mysterious ways. It will be like magic.

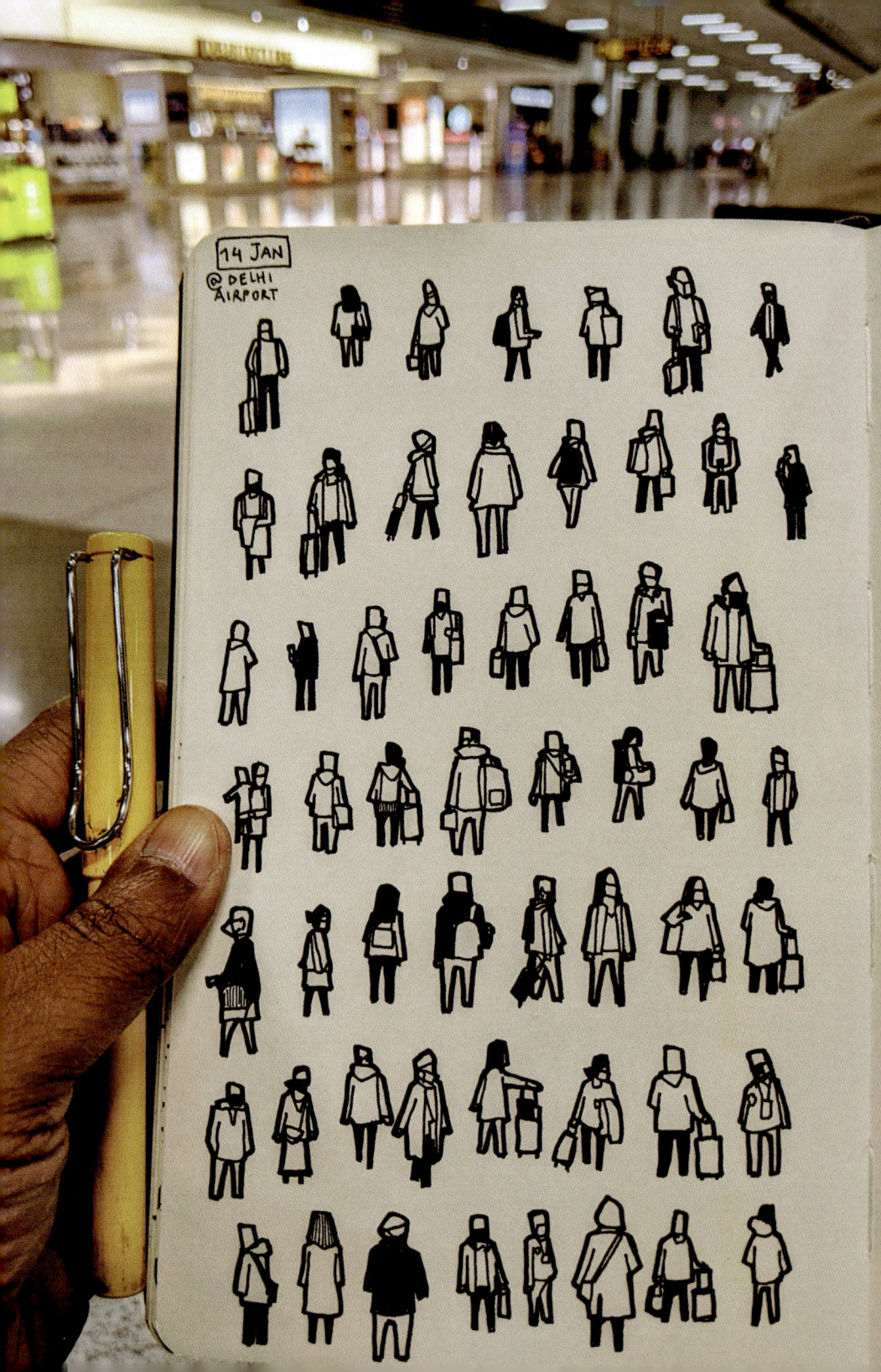

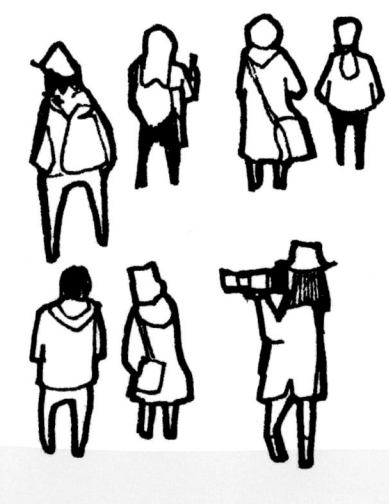

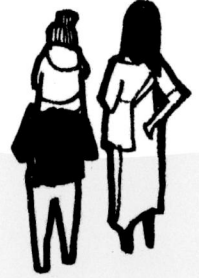

# CHAPTER 5
## SMALL IS BIG:
## DRAW TINY PEOPLE

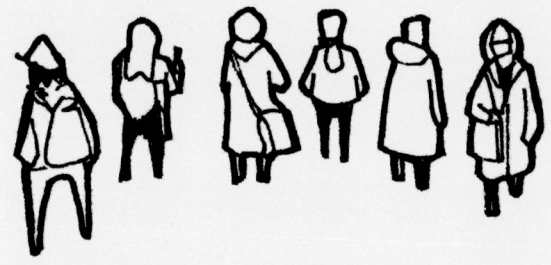

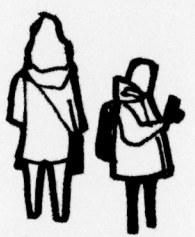

# A Five-step Guide to Drawing a Tiny Person

In the previous chapter I said that if you know how to write by hand, you already know how to draw, because writing and drawing are essentially the same thing. Strung together to form words and sentences, lines and shapes can express thoughts and arguments. Arranged on a blank page, lines and shapes can distill visual information of what is in front of you, what you notice about it, and how it makes you feel.

In this chapter, we will use our writing skills to directly inform our drawing skills. With the same shapes we use to write, we will draw some tiny people!

## STEP 1 >
## THE HEAD TELLS
## YOU WHAT THEY SEE

Shapes and sizes may differ, but a general head-shape can be a simple oval (like the English letter O), but with one end flatter than the others. Somewhere between capital letters O and D. How you draw the flat line tells where they are looking: up or down, left or right.

## STEP 2 >
## THE TORSO
## DETERMINES
## POSTURE

The torso is simpler than any letter of the alphabet. It is just a box! Leaning forward or back, tilting to one side or the other, the torso is a simple rectangle with a sprinkling of imagination. Squeeze it, twist it, stretch it, play with the basic shape and ask yourself, "What is this person doing, saying, and thinking?"

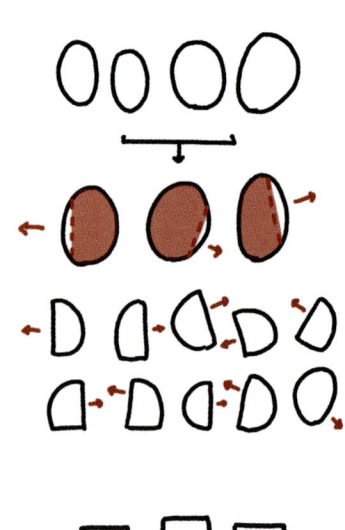

## STEP 3 >
## ARMS ARE FOR
## HOLDING THINGS

The simplest drawing of an arm is a rectangle again, but you can say much more with a simple tweak: tapering joints! The shoulder is wider than the elbow, and the elbow is wider than the wrist.

Still, arms can be difficult to draw. One way to make them easier is to give them something to do. Holding a coffee mug? Giving someone directions? Raised in passionate speech? Lowered in submission?

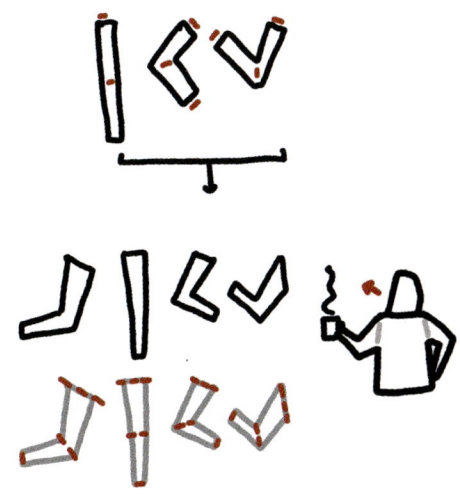

## STEP 4 >
## LEGS HELP THEM
## MOVE

Legs are good for helping us get around. Draw them like the bottom half of the English letter H and twist and tilt the shapes to move your tiny person. See what gives your tiny person a wider stance or a crouch or a walking motion.

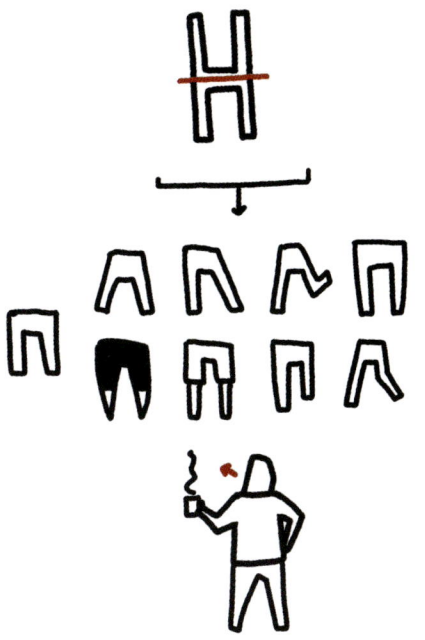

CONTINUED >

## STEP 5 >
## DETAILS ARE
## SIMPLE SHAPES TOO

When drawing in the real world, there is usually never enough time to get all the details right. Inevitably, you have to pick and choose what makes it to your page.

**The Ears** can be just the English letter C. Stretch it, shrink it, pull at one end—see what new shapes emerge from play. Ears are useful for indicating the direction someone is facing, and whether they are looking up or down.

**The Eyes** are dots. But if they wear glasses, I try to draw the glasses instead.

**The Nose** is the English letter L, tilting one way or the other, curved or sharp, big or small.

**The Mouth** is one of several simple shapes: the letter C lying on its back, the letter D lying one way or the other, simple triangles and simple rectangles. With these simple shapes you can convey joy, fear, anxiety, excitement, and so much more.

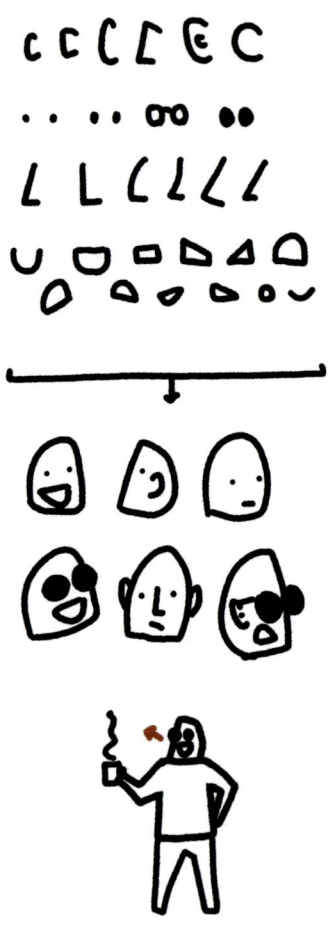

→  *Commuters at rush hour*

A drawing habit is the way to build a vocabulary of lines and shapes. Follow the cycle of observing and drawing, led by instinct and curiosity, and without wasting time on hesitations. Your lines will become *your* lines. Your shapes will become *your* shapes. Your drawings—made with your lines and your shapes—will look like no one else's. Only yours.

Play with the shapes we just learned and build your vocabulary. You will need them to find the tiny people of your world.

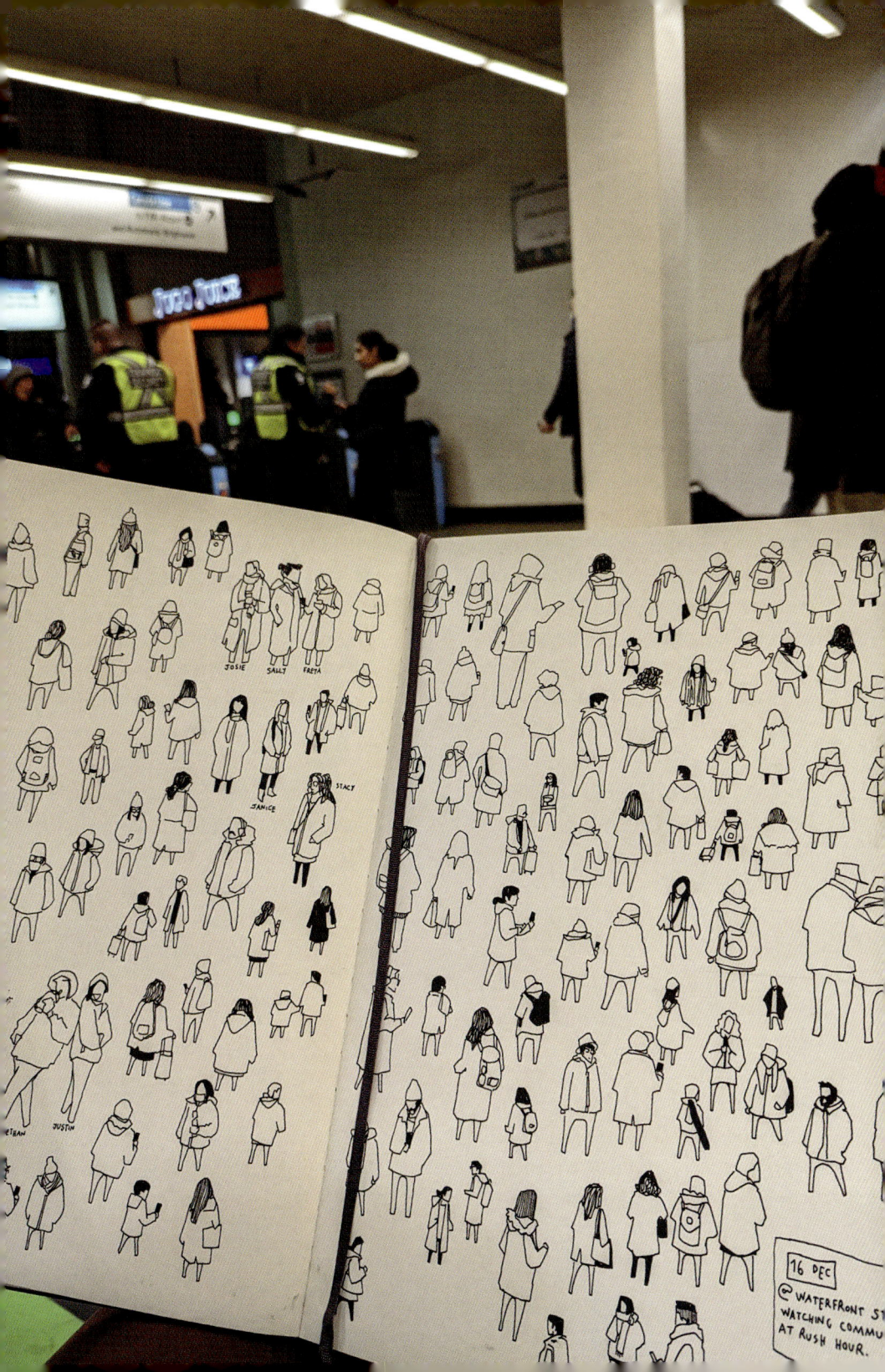

# Who Are Tiny People?

Tiny people are the countless, anonymous people of your world. They are the people who walk past you on the street, who sit at the other tables in the café. You see them on the bus and on the trains and outside your window. You may not recognize them as individuals—you may not even notice them at all.

I think of the word "sonder," described thus in *The Dictionary of Obscure Sorrows*: "the realization that each random passerby is living a life as vivid and complex as your own—populated with their own ambitions, friends, routines, worries and inherited craziness— an epic story that continues invisibly around you like an anthill sprawling deep underground, with elaborate passageways to thousands of other lives that you'll never know existed . . . ."

To observe the tiny people of our world is not to know everything about their rich and full lives, but to acknowledge that we are in the midst of a lot of great energy—that every day, in every place, worlds are colliding! Yours with theirs, theirs with yours, on and on to innumerable combinations, street after street, neighborhood after neighborhood, city after city.

Tiny people are tiny only because you know so little about them. Sometimes it is only the color of their coats or the sound of their shoes or the whiff of a conversation overheard. And even those things we soon forget, because the world is busy, and notifications distract us and useless information assaults our senses at all times of the day.

**To notice tiny people is a revolutionary act in distracted times.** It is a commitment to active observation. It is the decision to be present in your environment, unplugged from screens and devices. It needs you to shed judgments and preconceptions, to de-center yourself, and to appreciate the value other people bring to your world.

Tiny people make up your world, just like you make up theirs. Without them, your world would be quite empty. Without you, their world would be too. We are tied together

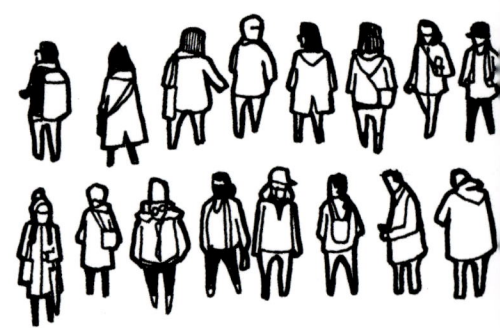

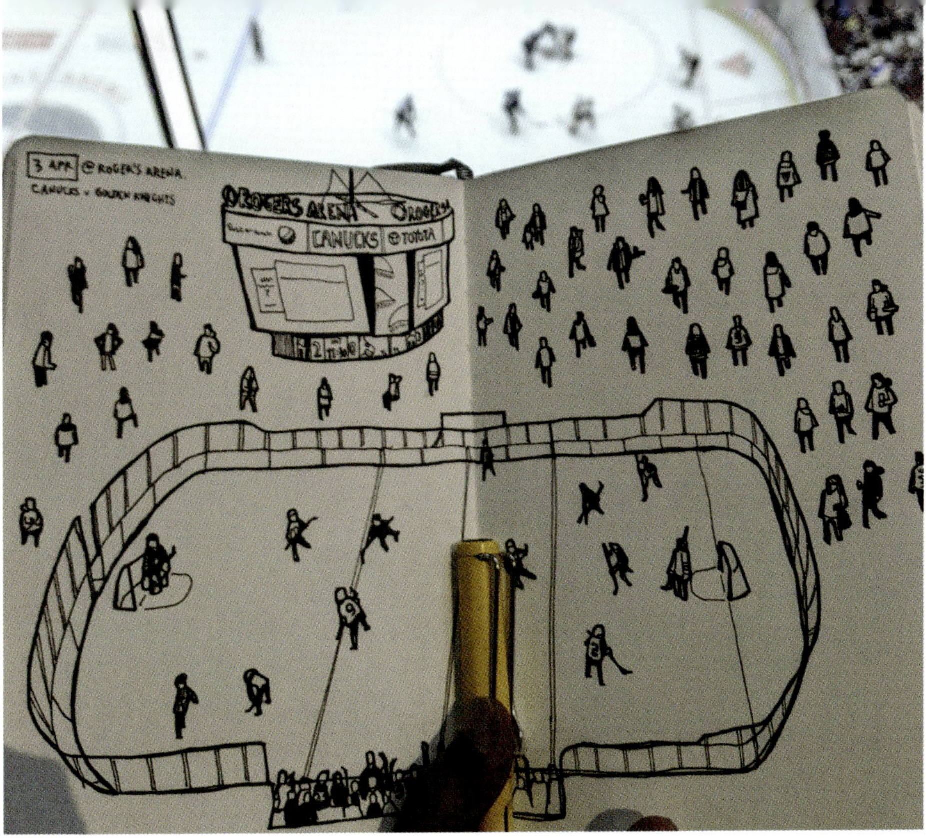

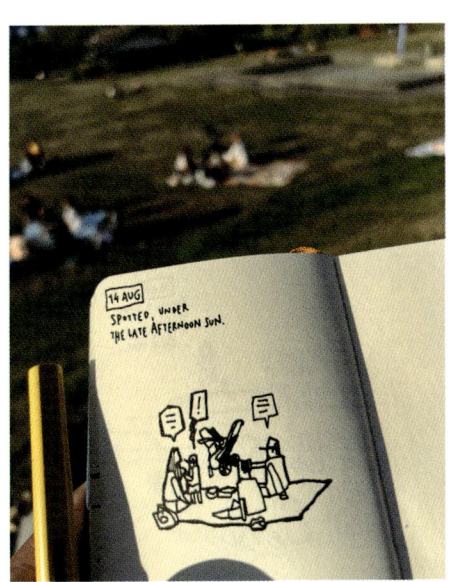

↑ *Capturing the hockey players and crowd*

in this, all of humanity, even though news and politics tell us otherwise. We are tied together in mutual coexistence, and it is a more beautiful world thanks to the presence of other tiny people in it. Thank you, dear reader, for being a tiny person in my world. I am glad to be in yours.

← *A family in the park under summer sun*

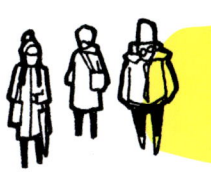

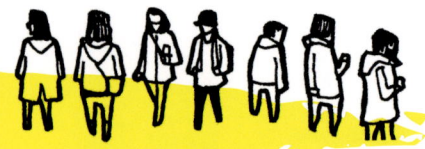

## How/Why I Started Drawing Tiny People

I was an immigrant in Chicago (USA) when I started to draw tiny people in a tiny sketchbook. I was looking for a way to understand these *crazy* people around me.

To be clear, the people of America are not crazy. But to the eyes of a newly arrived immigrant from India, they do exhibit odd behavior! The people of Chicago are independent, fiercely proud, and proudly unapologetic. They live their lives the way they want. They are dramatic, and everyone is the main character of their own TV show. It was a refreshing, challenging, and exciting thing to behold. *I did not know this was allowed.* So I looked for more people in other neighborhoods to confirm my findings. I was gathering clues for how I should be. I was trying to live among them, trying to fit in.

A sketchbook gives you superpowers. It taught me how to observe, but it also emboldened me to occupy space in a foreign world. The sketchbook became my license to sit at the café for an hour, to go to a bar by myself, to sit at a park bench

alone. It gave me a reason to watch life pass by. I was no longer concerned with how my drawings looked, because I was completely absorbed in the work of drawing itself. It began with searching, finding, seeing, and observing. It was fed by curiosity—about a pose, a dialogue, a dynamic between friends, a coffee table, a handbag, a traffic light. The lines had to be quick because my subjects were quick. They dropped into my world suddenly, and I had no time to lose because they could exit suddenly too. The only way to make this practice work was to give in to instinct and inspiration, to disregard hesitations and second thoughts—from one subject to the next and the next and the next . . . .

The more I drew, the better I felt. I grew comfortable in these foreign places. I connected, at a distance, with strangers across the street. Differences between people, between ourselves and others, are so easy to spot. But drawing is an act of attention that helps you see beneath the surface and go past the differences.

People are people, and tiny people can be quite large. What makes them tiny in my art is the minimalistic shorthand I developed, my own language and vocabulary for their eyes, noses, arms, and legs. Subconsciously, perhaps, I was

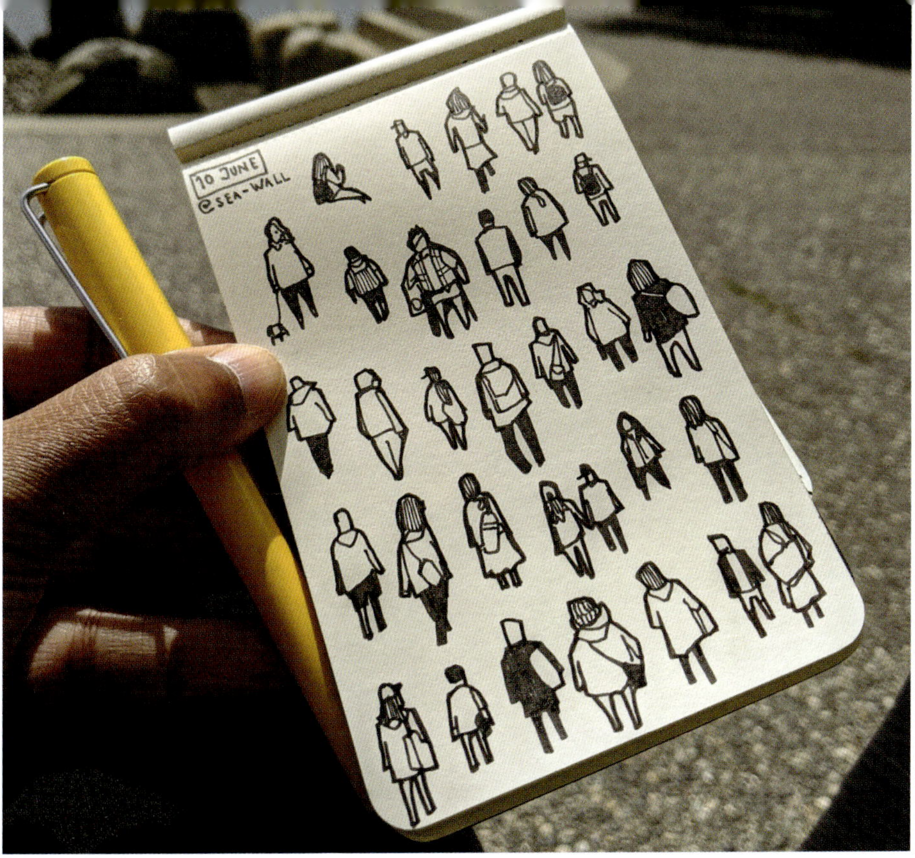

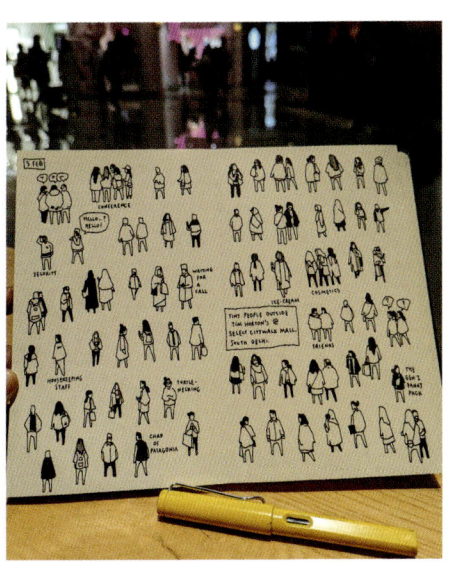

↑ *Sketching the tiny people who cross my line of vision*

looking to erase those details that separate us from one another. In trying to find common ground, in trying to draw them before they were gone, I found the essential features and characteristics that made them interesting, and made them just like me, or you, or anyone else anywhere in the world.

Your job as the artist is to also build a library of good lines and shapes, referencing your taste, your curiosity, and your tools.

← *At the mall*

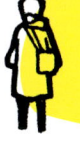

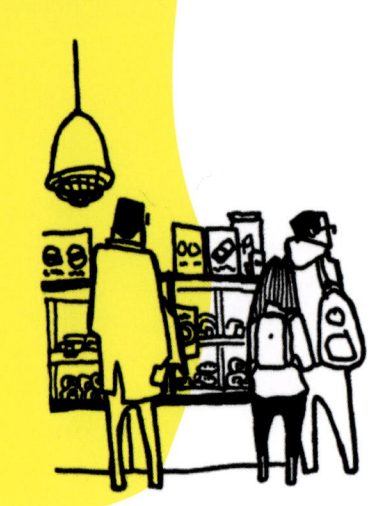

## Exercise:
## Drawing Tiny People at the Café

The friendly neighborhood café is a great place to start drawing tiny people.

Pick a comfortable spot. There are two kinds of comfortable spots for the anxious beginner:

1. **With your back against the wall**—so you can observe the other patrons without worrying about anyone peering over your shoulder.

2. **At the café window**—so you can see the people walking outside.

When facing indoors, your subjects are more stationary. They would be seated at the table, sometimes locked in conversation. When you look outside, your subjects are moving. Maybe they are at the traffic light? If so, can you draw them before they cross the street? Quick, there is never enough time!

Depending on where you sit, you can give yourself many fun and challenging goals.

> Draw the person at the front of the queue before they finish paying.

> Draw the people at the various tables, as if every table were an island of its own.

> Notice what people do with their hands when they are locked in conversation. Draw their posture leaning forward or back, notice their legs crossed or uncrossed under the table.

> Draw your coffee and the baristas behind the counter.

> Give stories to every table. What could they be talking about? What could be going on in their world?

To close the hesitation gap, set yourself a speed goal. Use a timer to give yourself sixty seconds from start to finish with each scene and figure.

Here are some good questions to think about: How big does a figure need to be for you to be able to complete drawing them in the allotted time? Does it help to draw smaller or larger? Remember, the goal is to finish drawing the figure, whatever it takes. Sometimes this is only possible if you skip over certain details. This editorial decision is yours.

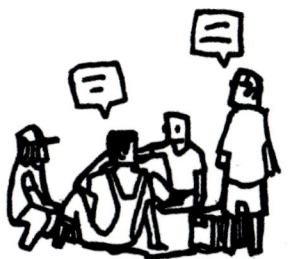

In doing this you will learn several things about yourself. For example, when confronting the ticking clock, which details did you immediately skip? Which details did you nevertheless always include? What does that say about what you notice and what you consider relevant? Where do your sketches begin: the head or the body or the table? What would happen if you changed this? Try starting at the feet and draw upward!

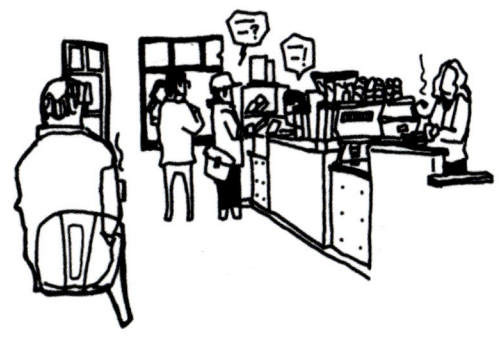

By following my curiosity, I learned that I care about how people interact with one another. I care about how we hang out with friends. I am curious about how we engage with public spaces (like cafés). I think about how we live our lives. And I like to discover the rules and norms that govern our behavior around other people (like queueing!).

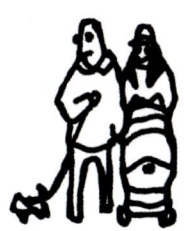

2 OCT

SINGAPORE.
LAND OF
MALLS.

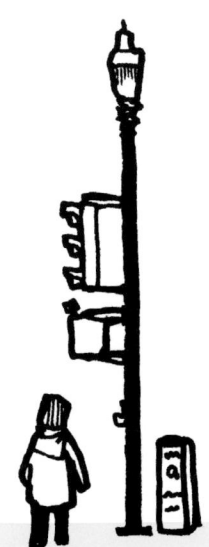

# CHAPTER 6
## THE FINISH LINE:
## HOW TO STOP

# The Other Big Obstacle

So I convinced you to open a sketchbook and not listen to hesitations and start drawing. Good job! But now we face the other big obstacle: how do you know when to stop? Your environment could be full of interesting things that demand a place on the page. You could become lost in the minute details. And then, inevitably, your time runs out or your bus arrives or your friends tap you on the shoulder to remind you the hike isn't finished yet, and you have to leave the drawing *unfinished*.

An unfinished drawing is still better than no drawing. But it does not give us that feeling of satisfaction we crave, the hit of dopamine that waits at the end of the process. And sometimes knowing you may not finish can discourage us from even getting started.

So this chapter is all about how to cross that finish line. It is about getting that dopamine hit. It is about holding up your sketchbook to the scene in front of you, taking a deep breath, and knowing that you did what you set out to do. Nearly as important, if (like me) you are often in the company of non-sketchers, it is about not exhausting the patience of your partner or friends!

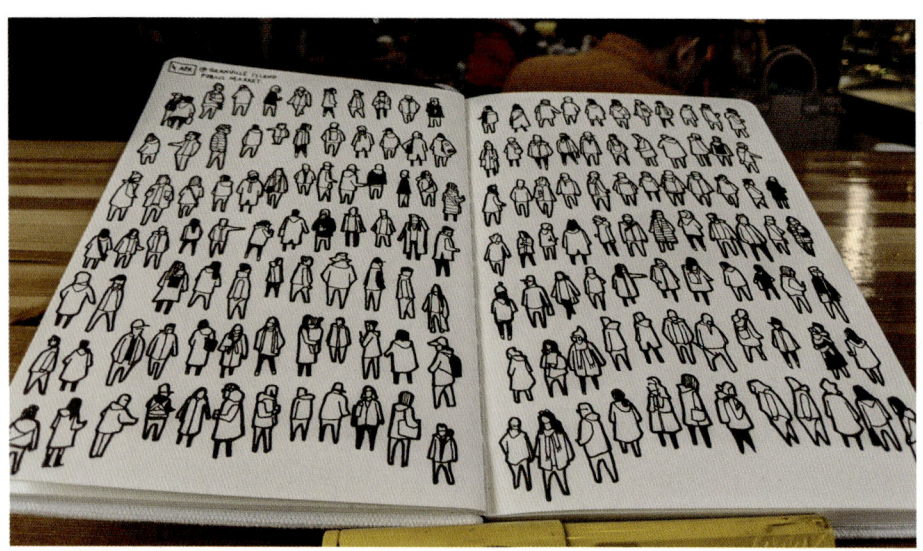

↑ *Filling an entire spread with tiny people. Each sketch only takes a moment and you can take as long as you like to fill the page.*

# Let Curiosity Guide the Way

Your curiosity reflects your taste and interests and tells you which direction to go. But, equally, it tells you where you do not care to go. You must listen to both signals.

You are the master of the little universe you create on the blank page. You are not obligated to anyone or anything else. But you must follow the lead of your curiosity. Not only does it do the big picture job of sustaining your sketchbook habit over weeks and months and (hopefully) years, it also lets you know where you want to give your precious attention.

Because a drawing is not only your skill displayed on the page but also a map of your curiosity and attention. Where did it focus? Where did it trail off? What did it return to? What did it ignore? The answers will be in your lines, shapes, colors, and subconscious editorial decisions. They will tell the story of you at that location, on that day, experiencing that weather, in the mood you were in. It is an abstract but powerful record of you in your world.

Know that you have the power to move toward the things you like, and ignore all else. This knowledge will give you the confidence to override hesitations when you want to draw but do not have enough time. This confidence will help you get started and, every single time, take you across the finish line.

Remember: You are the master of your page. Accept this responsibility. Exercise this power.

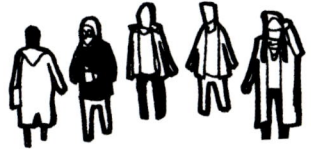

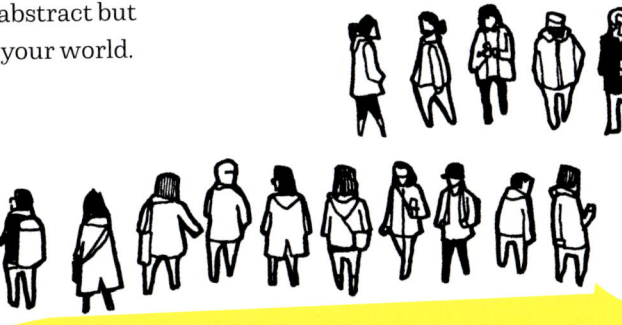

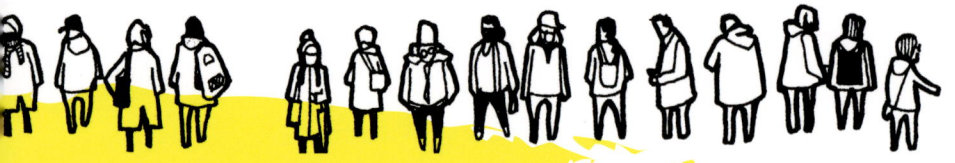

# Understand Your Circumstances

I love to draw wherever people congregate, around the hustle and bustle, with subjects constantly leaving and entering my frame of composition. I love to draw on buses and trains, but maybe my subject gets off at the next stop? I love to draw at the airport, but there is not a lot of time before boarding begins. I love to draw when sightseeing on vacation, but I am likely to be around civilians (non-sketchers!) who want to keep moving. To finish my drawings, I have to be ready for a sudden change in circumstances.

How do you know when a drawing is finished? There is no clear answer. It is the artist's job to decide when they are finished. In the following drawings, I had to start quickly if I wanted to draw. But in each case the idea of finishing was different. Sometimes it was purely my decision. Sometimes I had to let external factors persuade me. Each time, I was ready.

1. On Vancouver transit, I saw supports as frames enclosing my three very different subjects. With limited time, I focused on just the bare essentials until my stop arrived.

2. Waiting for my bus, I was intrigued by the various posts jutting into the blue sky. I saved time on the cars and focused on the posts.

3. In Singapore, the malls are so busy you could look at all the people all day, but I was entranced by the height of the interior space!

4. At the US-Canadian border, I was drawing a couple with their dog at the edge of the ocean when it began to rain. A drop made it to my page and smudged the ink, but I like to think it is a good marker of the weather that day.

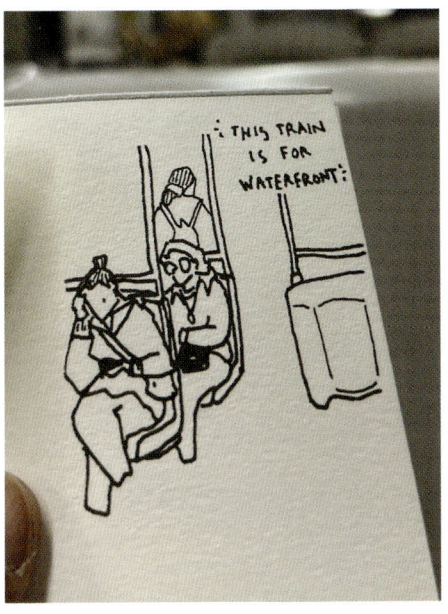

↑ *A quick sketch on the subway*

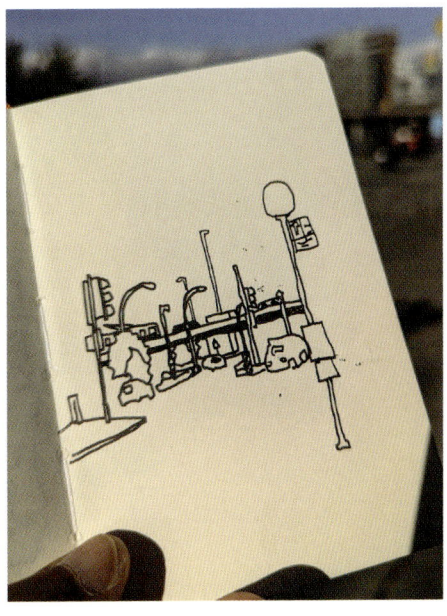

↑ *Even an unassuming street corner is an opportunity for a small sketch.*

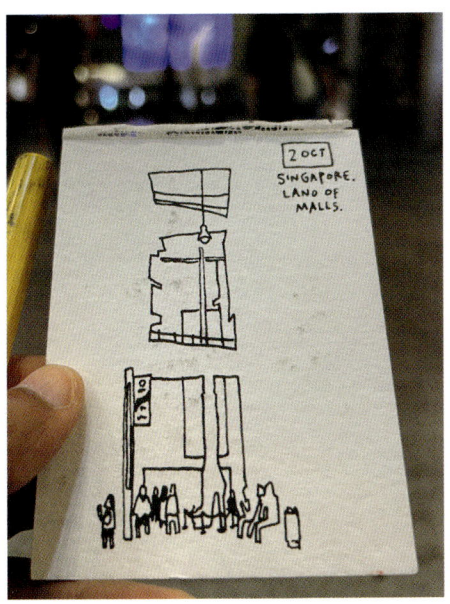

↑ *The hustle and bustle of Singapore mall life*

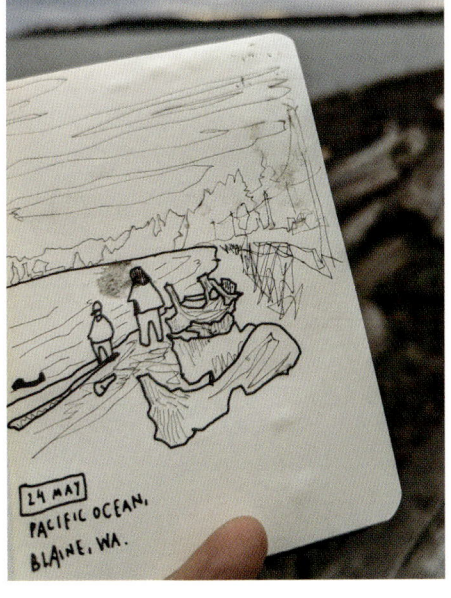

↑ *Sitting by water capturing a quick scene*

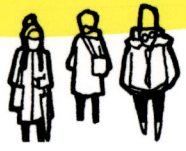

# Go Outside-In

In chapter 3, we used a curiosity spiral to begin from a point of interest and spiral outward. Just as this idea of going "inside-out" is useful at the macro level, the idea of "outside-in" is useful at the micro level to capture individual dynamic elements on your page.

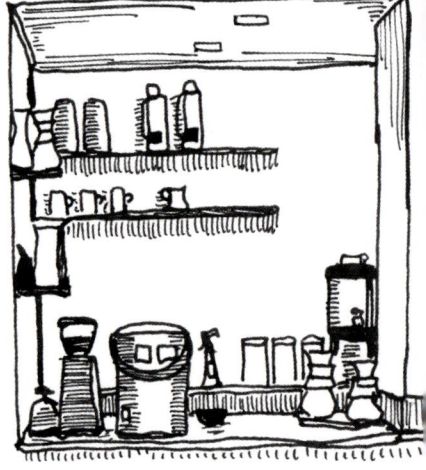

If you draw a busy street, or two people speaking at a café, or a boat floating past you, the subject of your interest is moving or changing swiftly. You should first capture the most dynamic aspect of your scene—a person's pose, the aspect of the ship as it approaches you, or the gait of a person walking by. The practice of going outside-in is about drawing the outer profile of your subject before going in for the various details.

Consider a couple at a café. What I find most interesting about them is their group dynamic—the way they lean toward or away from each other, the way they look at each other, and the movement of their arms and legs. There are other details about them that are interesting too, such as their hair or clothing or their coffee order, but those details will not change from one moment to the next.

So to capture this moment, it is important to begin with the outer silhouette of their bodies. Once this is done, I can focus on other details.

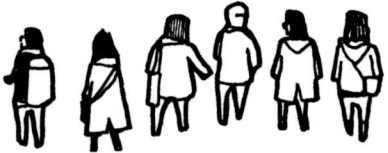

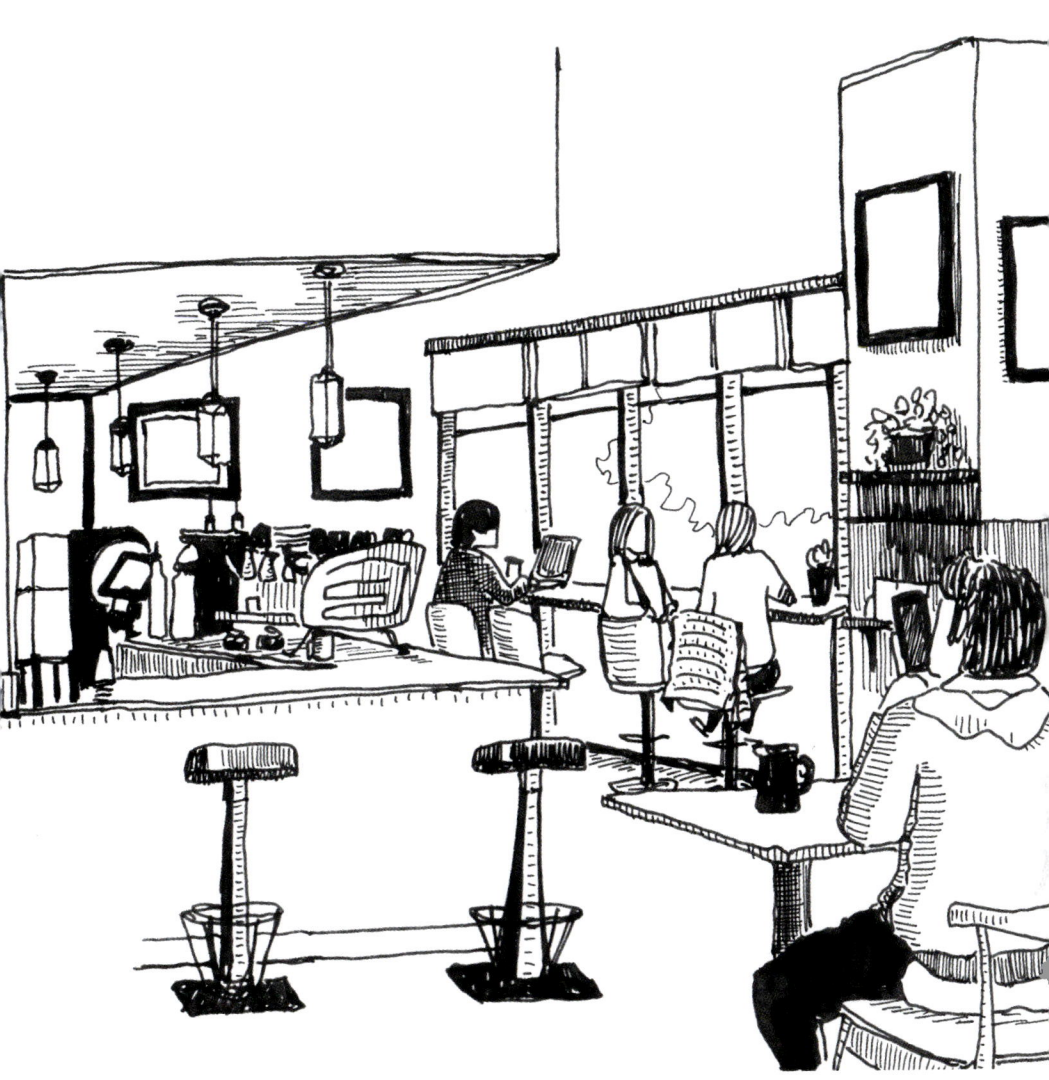

↑ *Learning to map interior spaces in Eau Claire, Wisconsin*

# Three Levels of Details

Separate the different elements of the page into three levels of importance, from the most detailed to the least detailed elements. Remember, there is no right or wrong answer—this is your decision based on how you feel.

The most detailed element holds the most information for a viewer, so they spend the most time looking at it. As the artist, this is also what you spend the most time drawing. So it should be the element most important to you—the subject that caught your eye, your reason to begin drawing.

The second level of detail is for important elements that support your subject. Maybe they give context to the place. Maybe they tell us what is happening. Maybe they establish the environment for your subject.

The least amount of detail goes to something that must be included but that you do not actually want to draw. There is always something like this in every busy scene! For me, often it is the trees and buildings. My subjects are usually humans because I am fascinated by human activity in public spaces. Trees and buildings are

## LEVEL 1

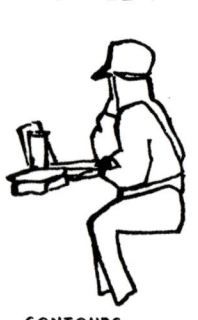

- CONTOURS
- QUICK SHAPES
- LONG LINES

## LEVEL 2

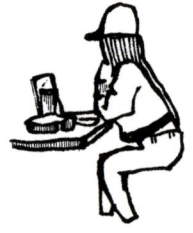

- KEY DETAILS
- MORE INFORMATION
- LIGHT and SHADOW

## LEVEL 3

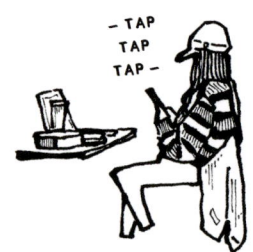

- MAX DETAILS
- PERSONALITY
- ACTIVITY DETAILS
- CLOTHING

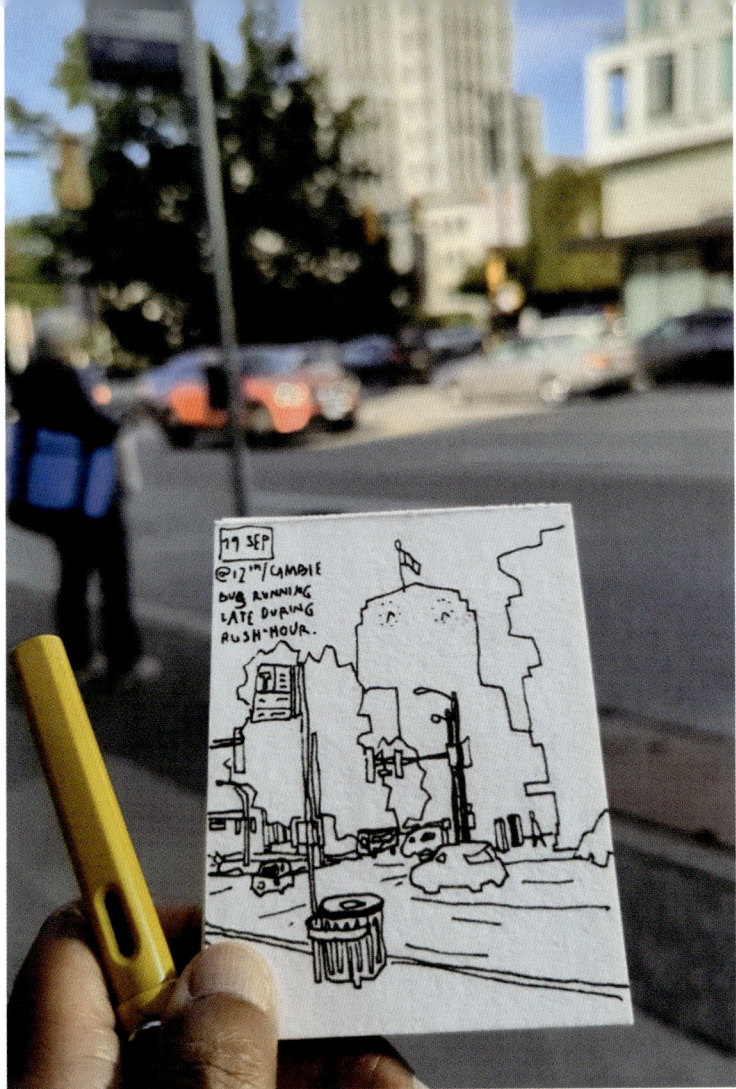

↑ *Running late, I only had time for a minimal sketch with few details.*

essential to describe the urban space, but I do not like drawing them. So I draw their outer silhouette, enough to suggest the size and general shape, and leave it at that.

You might think this is a cop-out. You may say I have no business drawing an urban scene if I don't want to draw buildings. But this is part of taking pride and ownership of your work. Your page is your page. Mine is mine. We get to make these decisions for ourselves.

# Why Three Levels?

There are two important reasons to use three levels of detail in the elements on your page. Let's talk about them here.

### Reason #1:
### It Creates a Hierarchy of Importance

When everything on a page is equally detailed, nothing stands out. Different levels of detailing, however, subliminally inform the viewer about what you want them to see, and help them better understand your focus, your interests, and the purpose of your art. At the same time you are also creating a visual journey for them to travel across your scene.

### Reason #2:
### It Helps You Finish

When you have less time, you cannot afford to give equal amounts of time to every element. Establishing different levels of detail allows you to complete complex scenes in less time. Knowing that you can do this makes it easier to get started when you really want to draw, and there is a lot to see, but you do not have a lot of time.

There is a third reason why it's important to use three levels of detail. It is in the next section because, well, it deserves its own space.

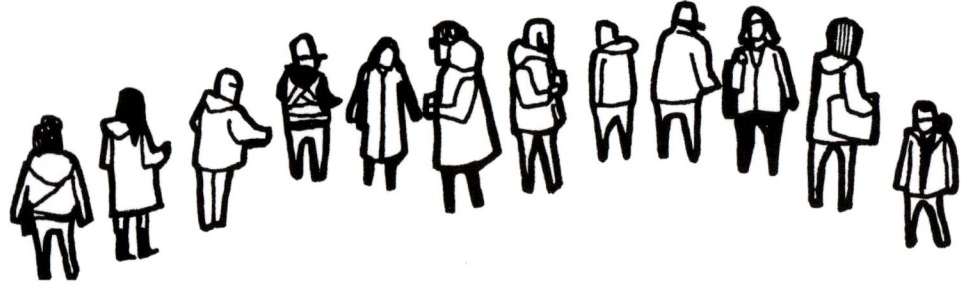

# You Are the Filter

The great value of your art is that it reflects you, the artist, and that your page be the most authentic representation of who you are. But for that to happen, you have to stop hiding yourself. The path to style, the path to joy, the path to a sketchbook habit that makes you more observant and mindful and attentive, requires your utter honesty before the page. This is the third important reason for using three levels of detail in your art.

How you see the world is filtered many times before your hands make lines and shapes on the page. The first filter is your eyesight and what you are able to see. After that, the filters are those of your mind—your taste and your personality. The filter is you. And when you give yourself permission, your mind works in harmony with your body, and inside every page you can find yourself.

There will be expressions of ideas that you never put into words. There will be feelings you did not express, not even to yourself. The page will tell you what matters to you, even if it is something as trivial as whether you care for architecture or the shape of a particular car. When you had to finish quickly, what did you skip? When you were pressed for time, what did you

nevertheless make sure to include? You will discover what matters to you.

A sketchbook is a gift you give yourself in this busy, distracting, complicated world. Every page reveals yourself to you.

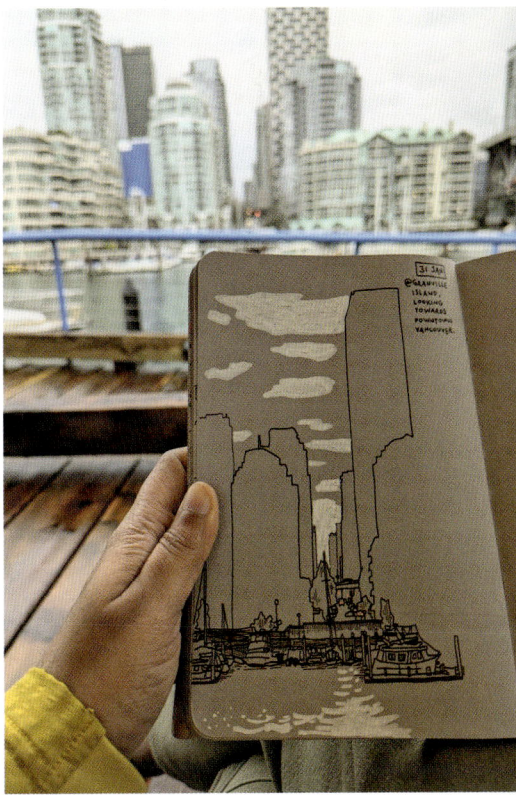

↑ *Can you tell I don't like drawing windows?*

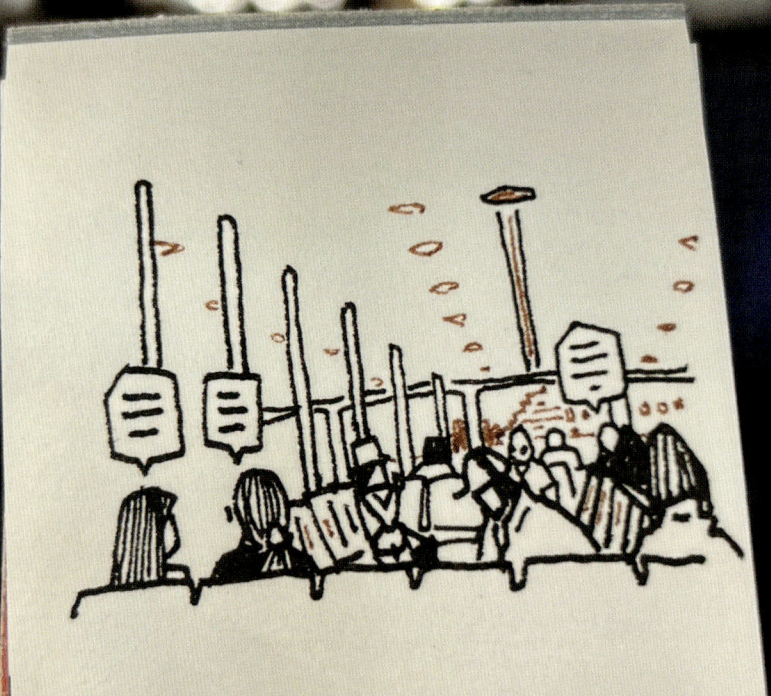

10 MAY

ON THE
SEA-BUS.

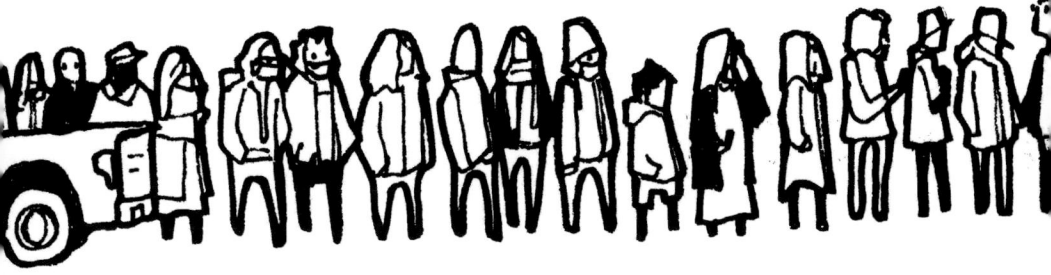

# CHAPTER 7

**THE GIFT
OF ATTENTION:
FINDING INSPIRATION
IN YOUR WORLD**

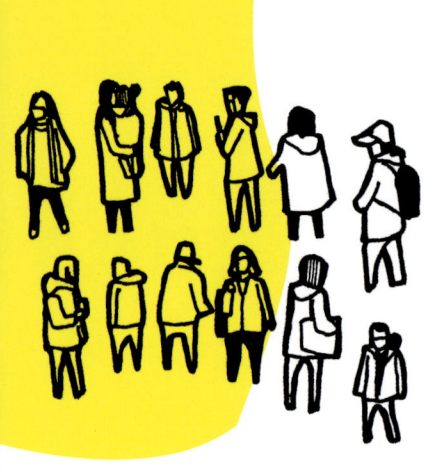

## Seeing Through a Sketchbook

I did not want to write a book simply to help people become better at drawing other people or lampposts or trees or buildings. There are already innumerable books, tutorials, and teachers to help with that, and they can probably do a better job than me.

A sketchbook habit made me into an artist, even though I did not set out to become one. But before the conscious decision to be an artist, it taught me how to let go of the distractions of our modern existence and really be in my world, and really see my world. I wrote this book so I could help you see too.

Seeing is not merely a matter of eyesight . . . it is a matter of where we give our attention. Today, it takes a supreme effort of will to freely give our attention where we want. We have to overcome the distractions orchestrated by billion-dollar companies to fragment our attention spans, to isolate us from one another, and turn us into perfect consumption machines for the things they want to sell.

The internet, the technology in our phones, and everything else that was supposed to set us free has enslaved us. Our world has never been more interconnected, yet at the same time, we have never been more lonely. In this silent pandemic of our lives, we scroll, tap, record, and post, to feed the algorithms our reality, even while we starve ourselves.

But I want to tell you that it does not have to be this way. The goal of this book is to help you reconnect with your world. To reestablish relationships with our local environments and the people with whom we share them. We live in a beautiful world with countless beautiful people.

I want to show you how attention and observation can help you become a part of your world again. To live not as a passive consumer but as an active human in a rich, beautiful world again.

All you need is a sketchbook.

The job of the artist, I would come to realize, is not to depict beautiful things but to find the beauty in all things. This beauty is sometimes not on the surface, invisible at first glance. It is the artist's eye that must go beyond the first glance, plumb deeper than the surface, in order to unearth it. It is the artist's job then to share this beauty with others, so that they might see it more easily. Living in the middle of the Midwest taught me to do this.

I learned that beautiful things are everywhere, hiding in plain sight, waiting to be seen. I learned that surface beauty can distract us, prevent us from seeing the *real thing*. It pleases so easily, that you need not do the necessary job of paying deep attention. Attention uncovers real beauty. And if you train your eye to pay attention, suddenly you will see it everywhere. Once you know how to see it, nothing can stop you.

Drawing in Wisconsin helped me as an immigrant. It helped me look past the surface differences between other people and myself—those differences were so easy to spot. It helped me appreciate other people at a deeper, more human level, the level at which we are all more alike than we know, in which we are all moved by the same forces—happy, curious, thirsty, playful, lazy, in the same ways.

Sitting in a café with people who looked nothing like me, I could see them order the same coffee as me, lean forward to talk the way I did, laugh as I did, and return their plates with the same care that I would. Suddenly, and even at a distance, I could connect with the strangers of my New World.

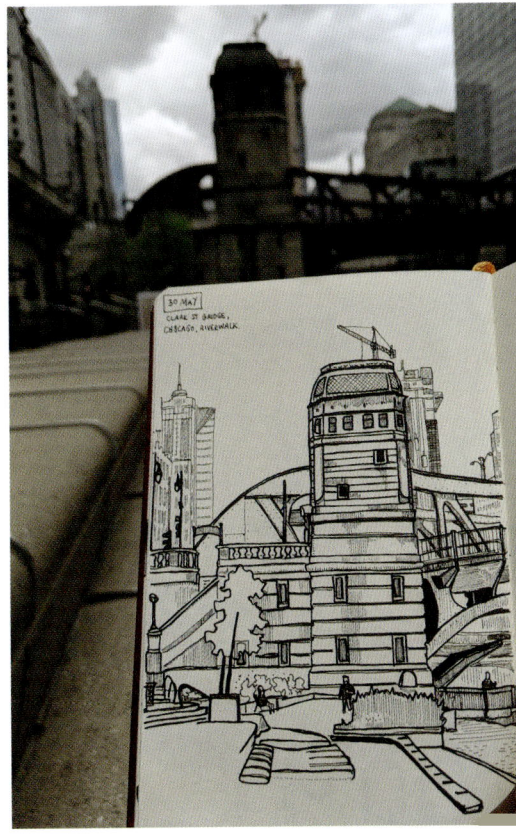

↑  *The essential lines of Chicago architecture*

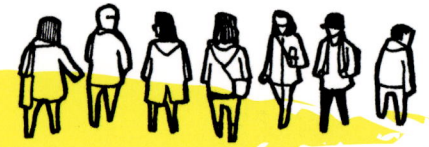

# Tips for Drawing in Outdoor Spaces

My sketchbook habit began in Chicago, one of the most beautiful cities in the world. It was easy to find great beauty, and inspiration was around every corner. But soon after, we moved to a town in the middle of the American Midwest, and it was not so easy anymore.

To find beauty in my environment, I had to look carefully at the ordinary things, the unremarkable streets, and the everyday moments of life. This was my challenge, but also my blessing. Living in wonderful Eau Claire (Wisconsin), I realized that beauty is everywhere, hiding in plain sight. It needs us to pay attention, and sometimes it needs us to look, then look again.

Go out with your sketchbook, without an agenda or destination. Let your eyes see everything, and your mind connect with its curiosity.

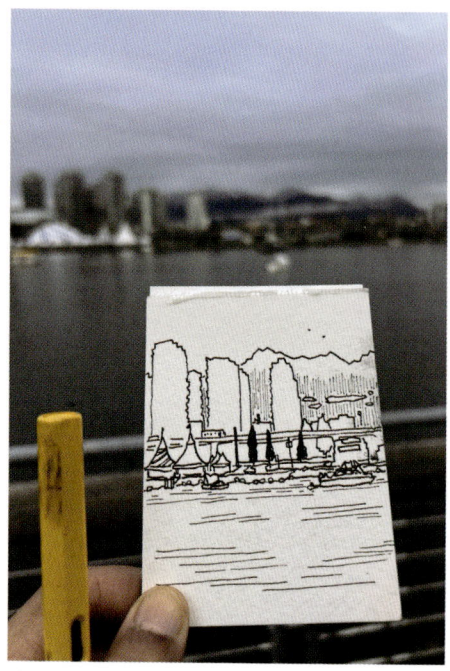

**FIND A SPOT**

When you see something, find a comfortable spot to sit or stand. You do not want to change positions too much, and you want a good view. (And if you are a sneaky artist too, you want to be inconspicuous. Make it a good, but sneaky, view!)

↑ *Up-close and far away views in Vancouver*

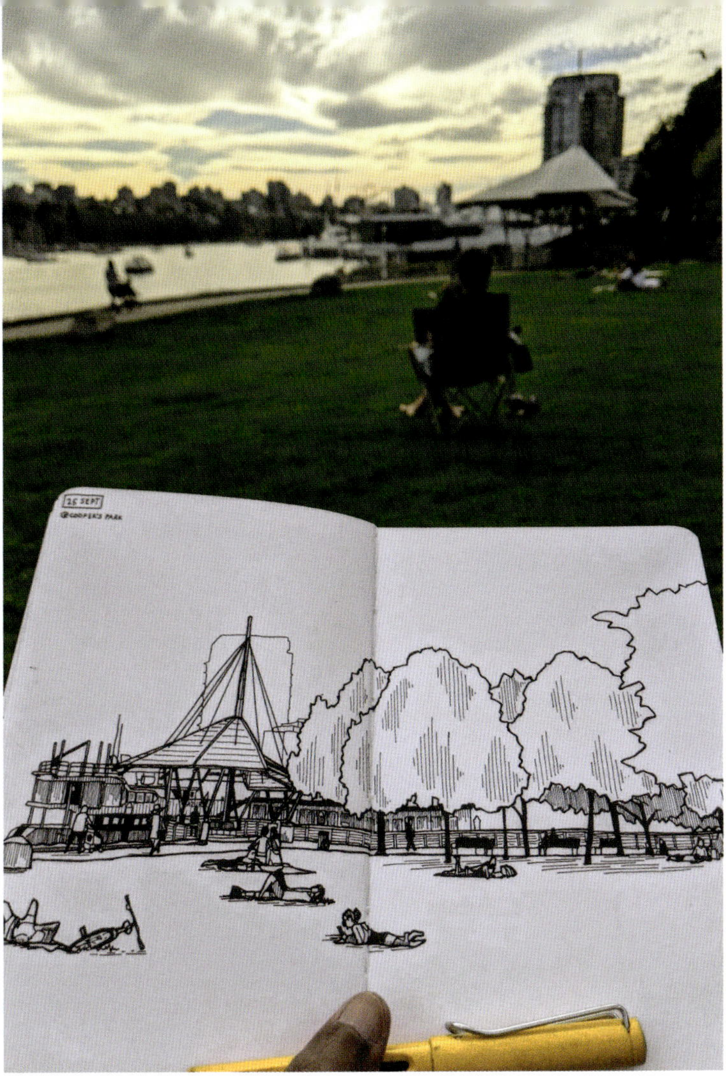

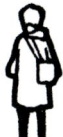

## LOOK FOR CLUES

Think not only about your subject of interest, but also the little clues that explain this landscape: lampposts, sidewalks, traffic lights, trees, benches.

↑ *People lounging under a summer sun, Vancouver*

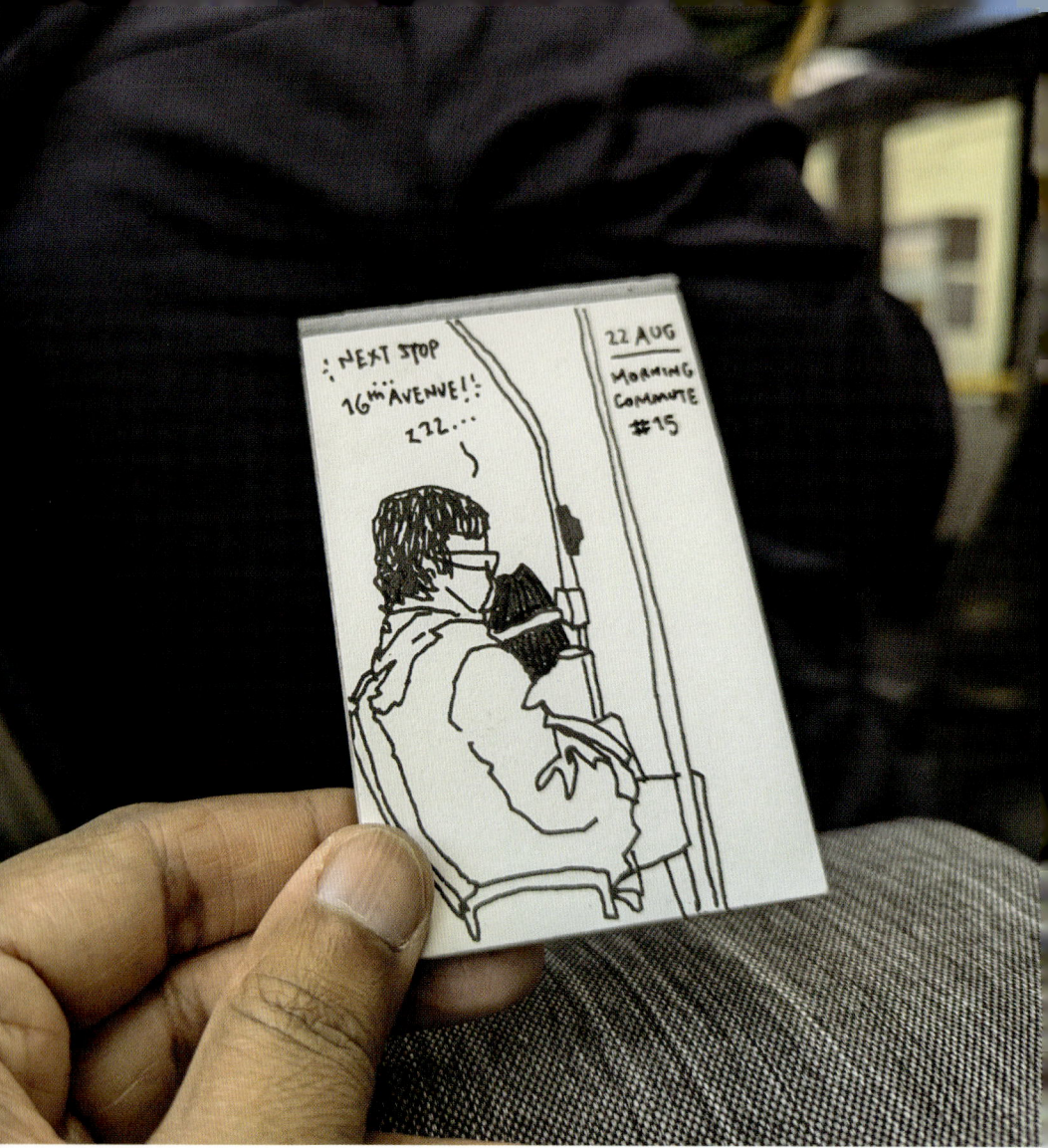

## GO WITH THE FLOW

Embrace the fleeting nature of
our dynamic world—a constantly
changing scene is Hemingway's
moveable feast; use it as inspiration
to give up the illusion of control, and
embrace your imperfections.

↑  *The morning commute*

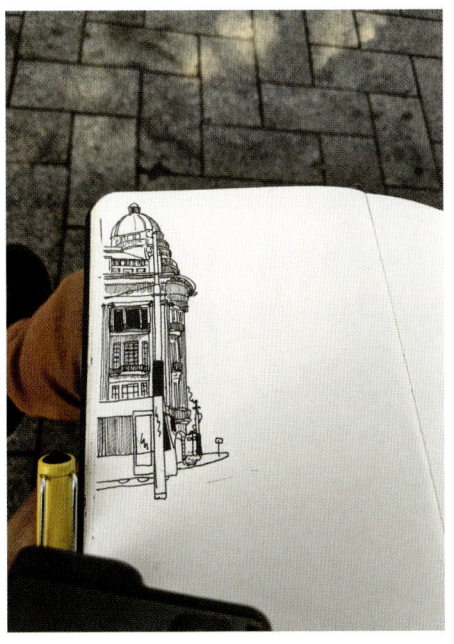
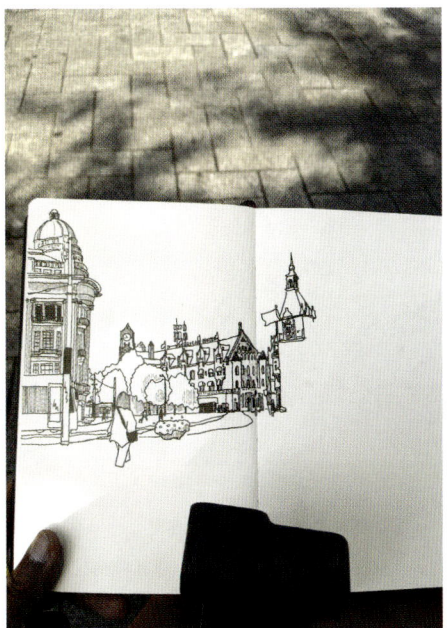

↑ *Drawing a scene in Amsterdam, working from the left side of the scene to the right*

**SNEAKY ART TIP #127**

When using ink, begin by drawing something that helps you draw the next thing. Hop across the page like that, using one element to scale and reference the next. In the step-by-step illustration, notice how the page builds from left to right from this principle.

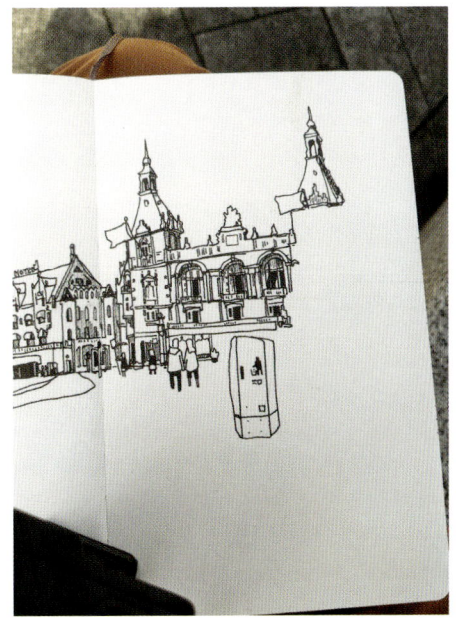

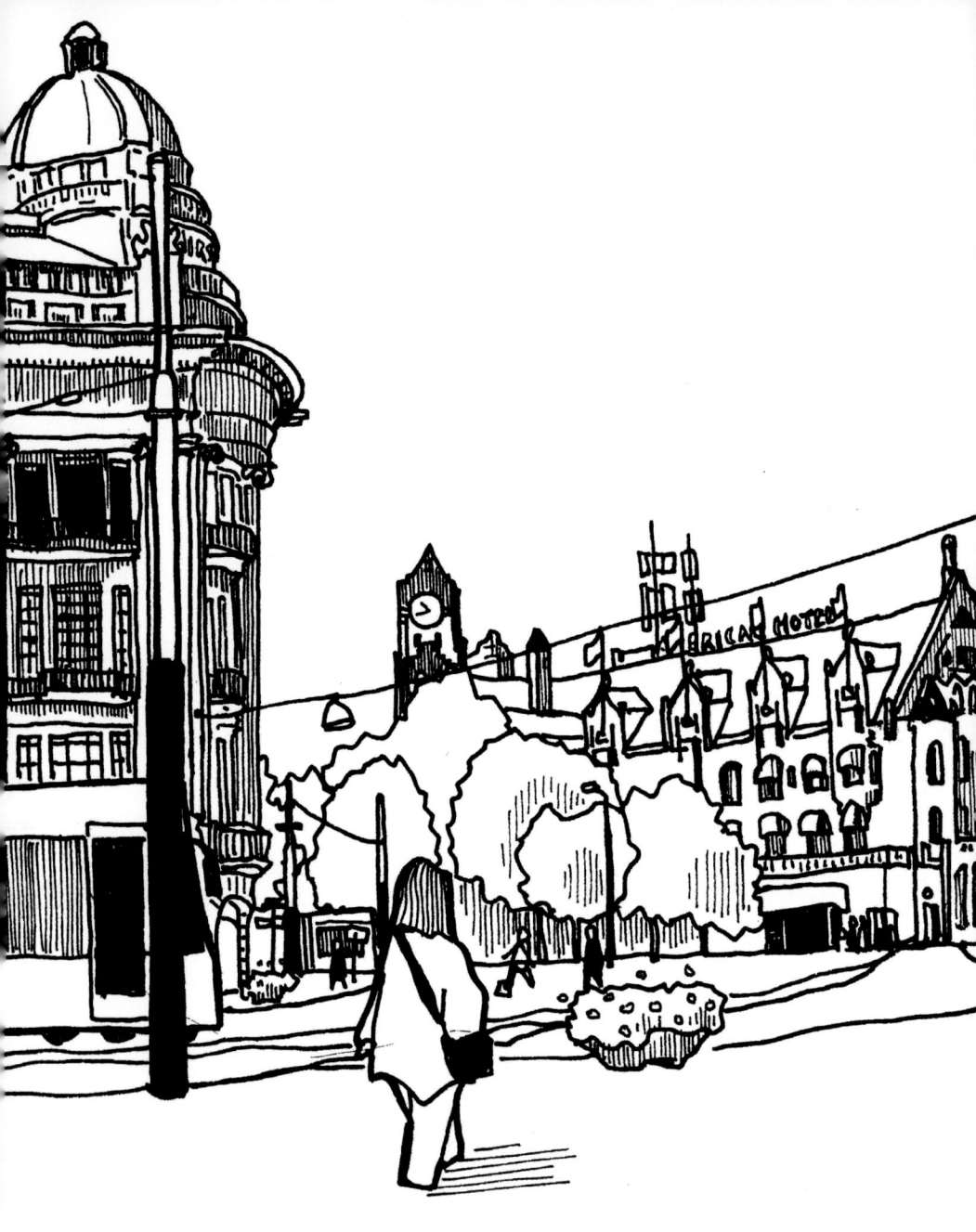

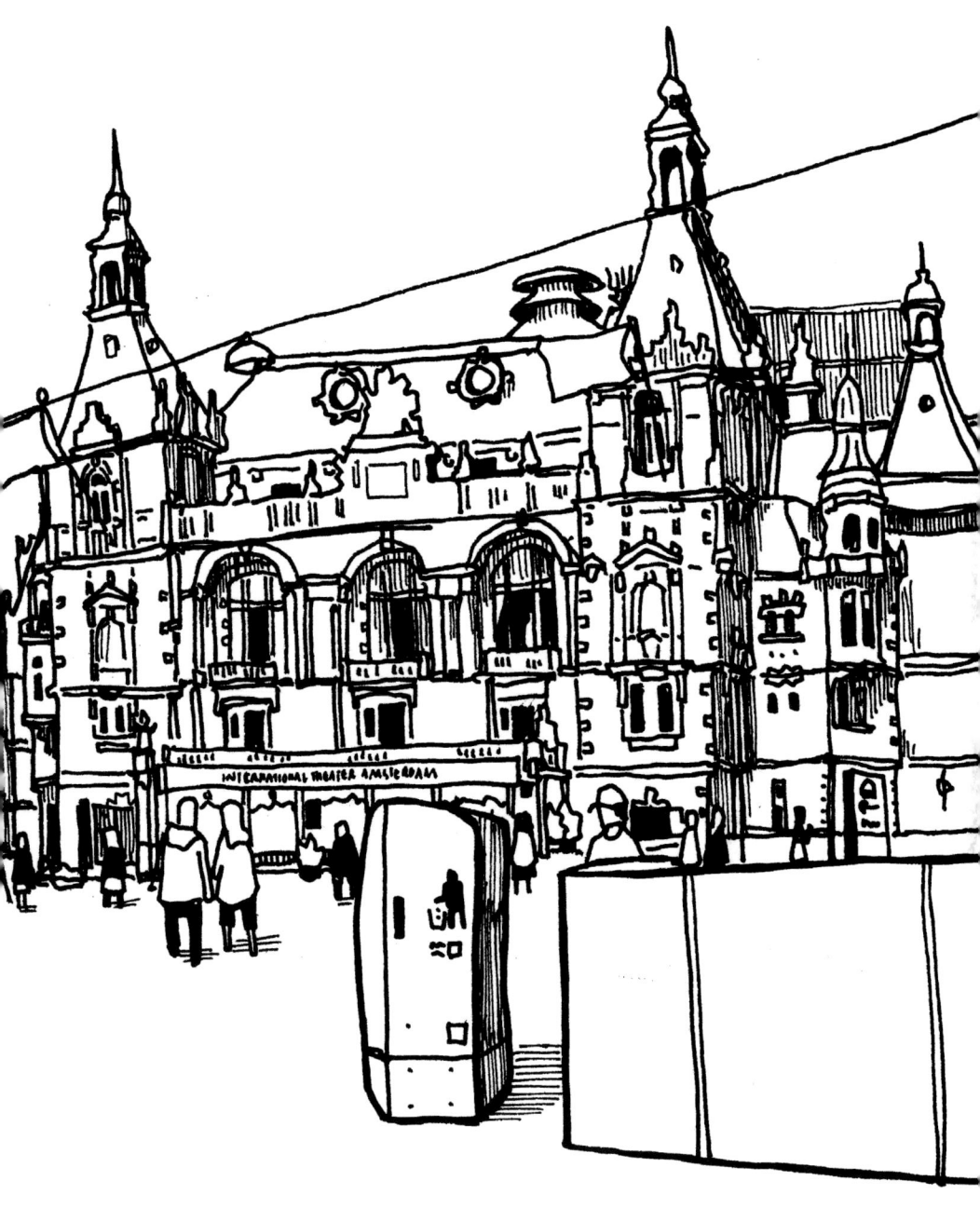

↑ *The finished sketch*

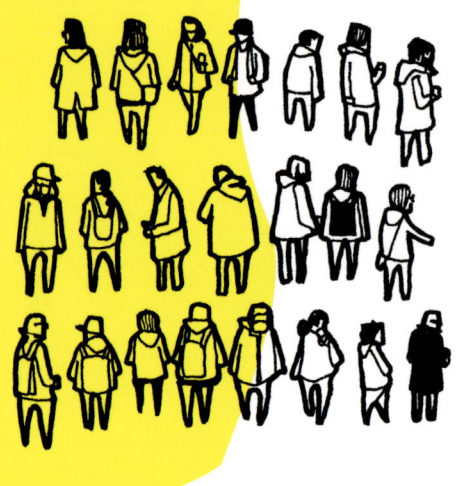

# Tips for Drawing in Indoor Spaces

Indoor spaces are defined by their decor, the various people we find there, and the things they do. Once you begin noticing these things, you will always find something worth a sketch.

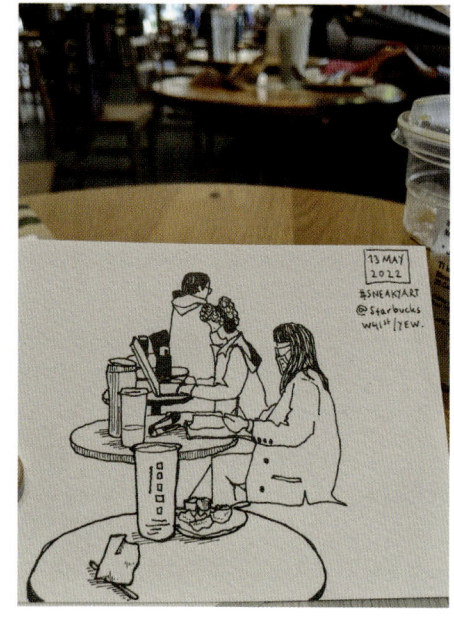

↑ *Corner seat at a Starbucks in Kerrisdale, Vancouver*

## TAKE THE CORNER SEAT

To the self-conscious sketcher, a corner seat provides the reassurance that no one can peer over their shoulders. Maybe then we can finally stop overthinking and get into the drawing?

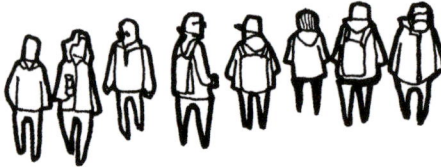

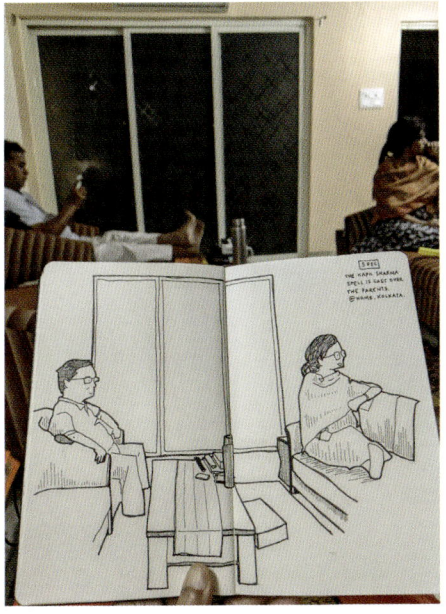

↑ *How my parents sit at home when watching TV*

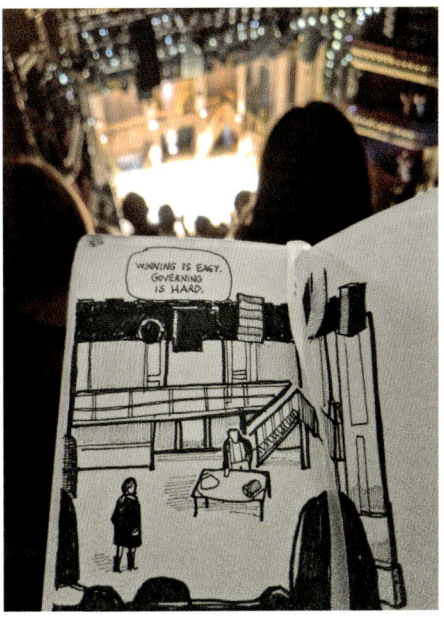

↑ *Watching a production of Hamilton at the CIBC Theatre in Chicago, 2019*

## NOTICE HOW THINGS ARE USED

When drawing at your—or another person's—home, notice the unique details that mark this space and how they are used. For example, I am always curious about furniture arrangements in people's homes and how they fit into their daily usage.

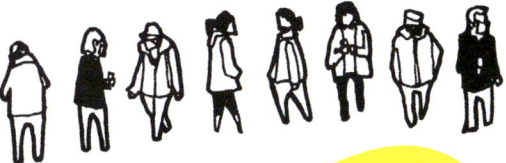

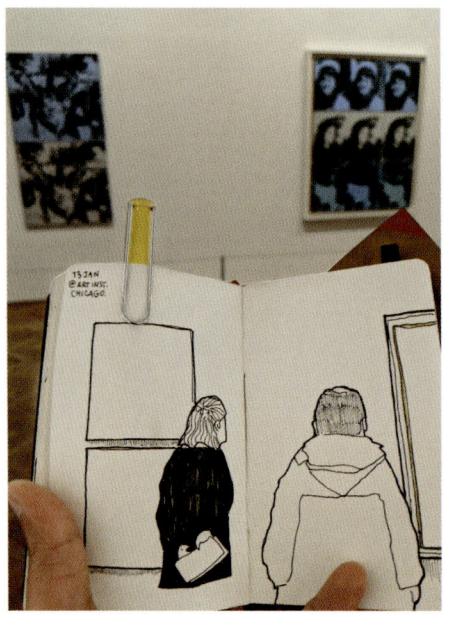

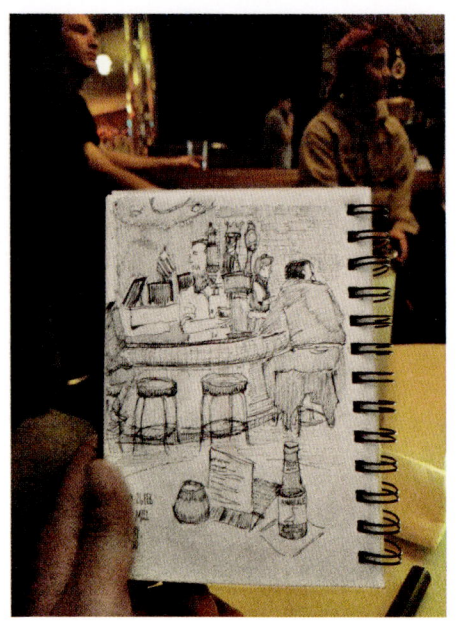

↑ *Empty frames and excited watchers at an Andy Warhol exhibit in the Art Institute of Chicago*

↑ *Darkness as subject when the poetry begins at the Green Mill, Chicago*

## FIND THE FRAME

What gives an indoor location its sense of space? What makes it small and cozy, and what makes it grand and spacious? Are there elements that enclose our subjects, as if framing their form and actions?

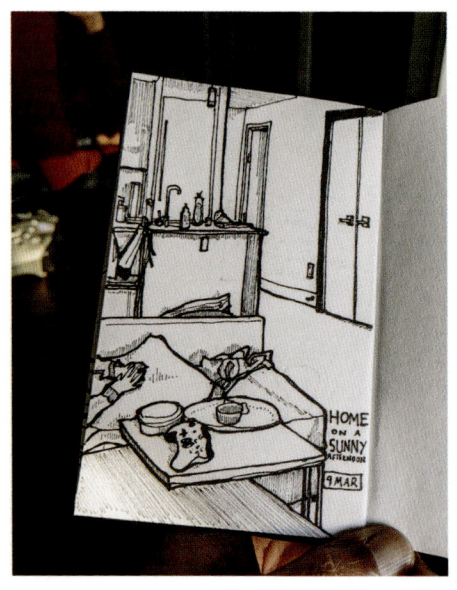

→ *Changing my seat on the couch for a "fresh" view*

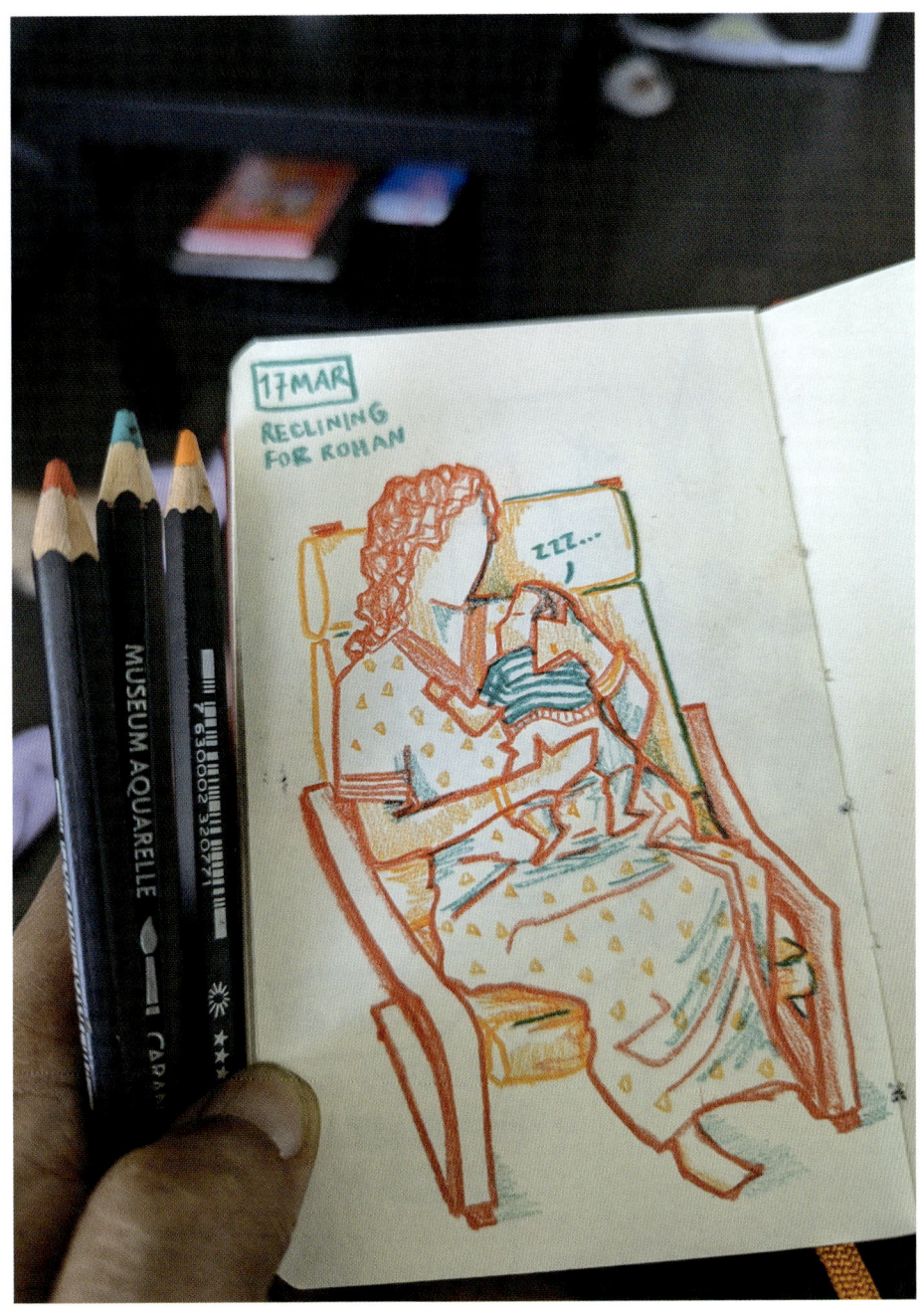

↑ *The recliner as frame?*

THE GIFT OF ATTENTION: FINDING INSPIRATION IN YOUR WORLD 97

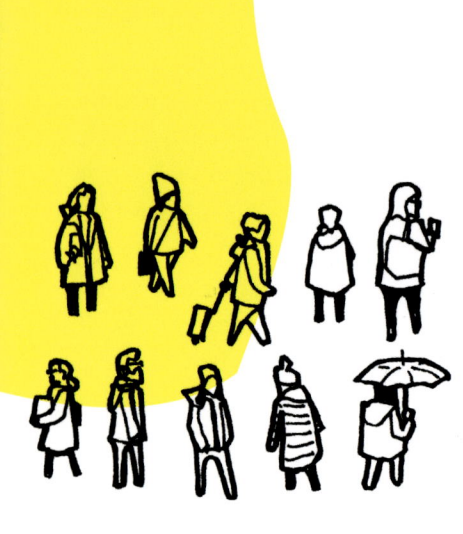

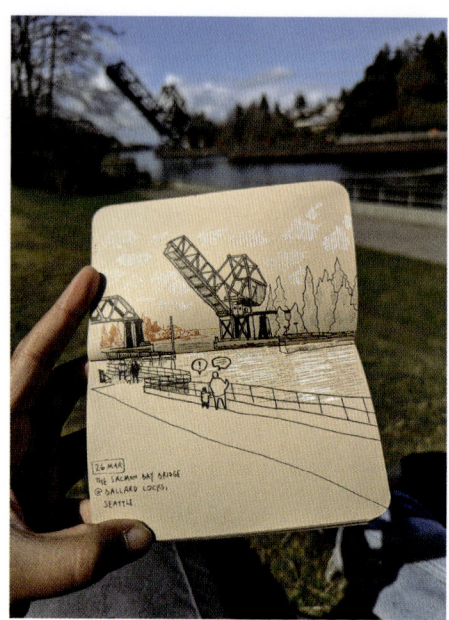

# Tips for Drawing While Traveling

Travel is a time of great situational awareness. We are naturally eager to see new things and discover interesting sights. We are also in the frame of mind to record what we find. But travel is also often done with others. And it may be inconsiderate to take up too much time at one location after another, sketching away while they wait! So use travel as an opportunity to draw, but move fast and draw simply. What tools help you achieve this end? What is the right mindset?

## SIZE MATTERS

Carry a smaller sketchbook— something that fits in the palm of your hand can be good to capture moments quickly when on the move.

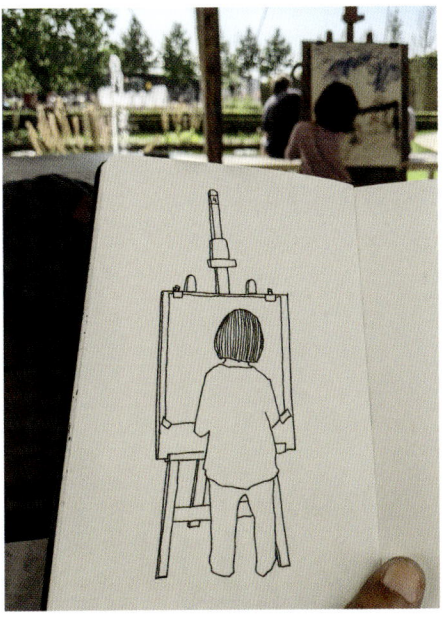

↑ *Young artist at play!*

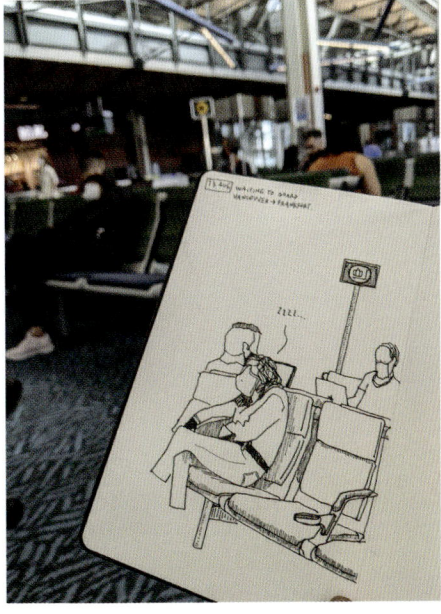

↑ *Late-night flight*

## SIMPLE ART OF THE SIMPLE THINGS

Find the little things—you will not always have a lot of time for detailed drawings, so maintain the habit by making simple drawings.

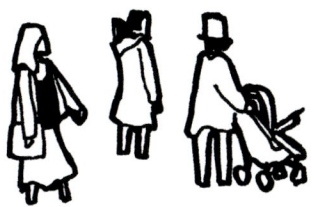

## THE SKETCHBOOK AS ALBUM

Keep a separate sketchbook for every vacation—even if you have pages left over at the end, a sketchbook for every vacation is a private space forever linked with the trip. Open it afterward and you will unlock all the things you saw, heard, and felt, even the memories that did not make it onto the page. It's the magic of a sketchbook!

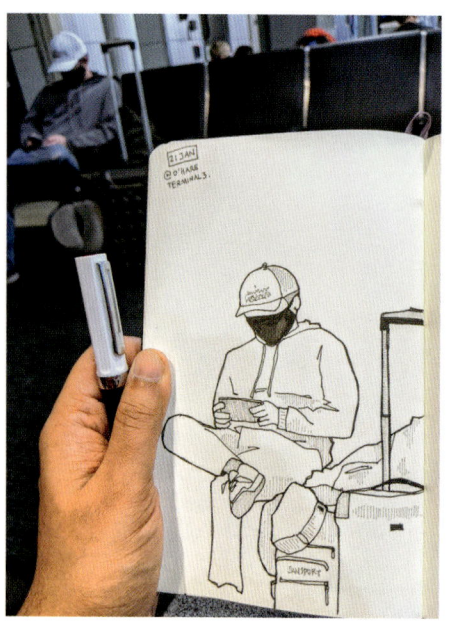

↑  *Waiting to board*

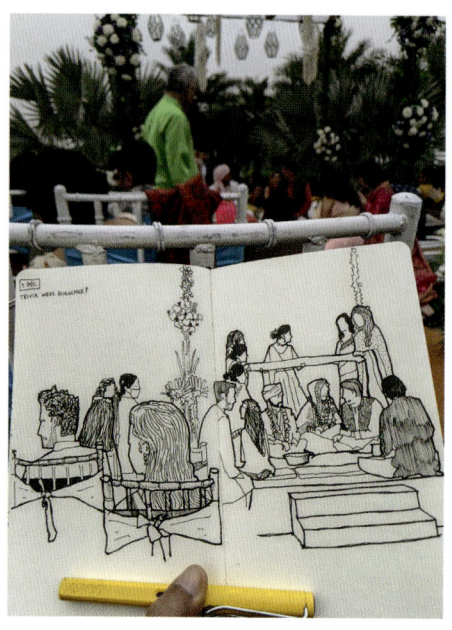

↑  *A close friend's wedding ceremony,*
   *New Delhi, India*

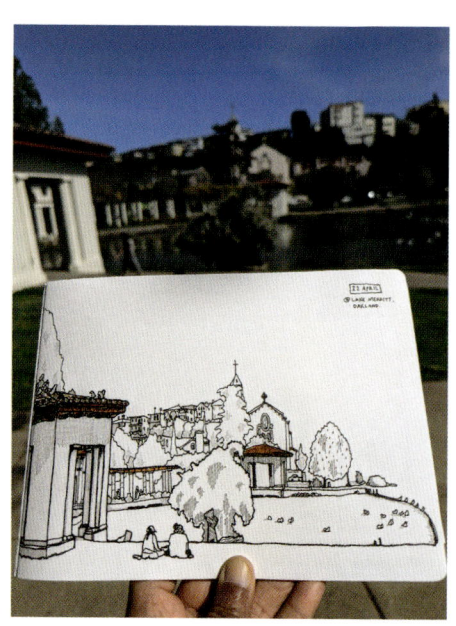

→  *People and ducks enjoying the*
   *weather, Oakland, California*

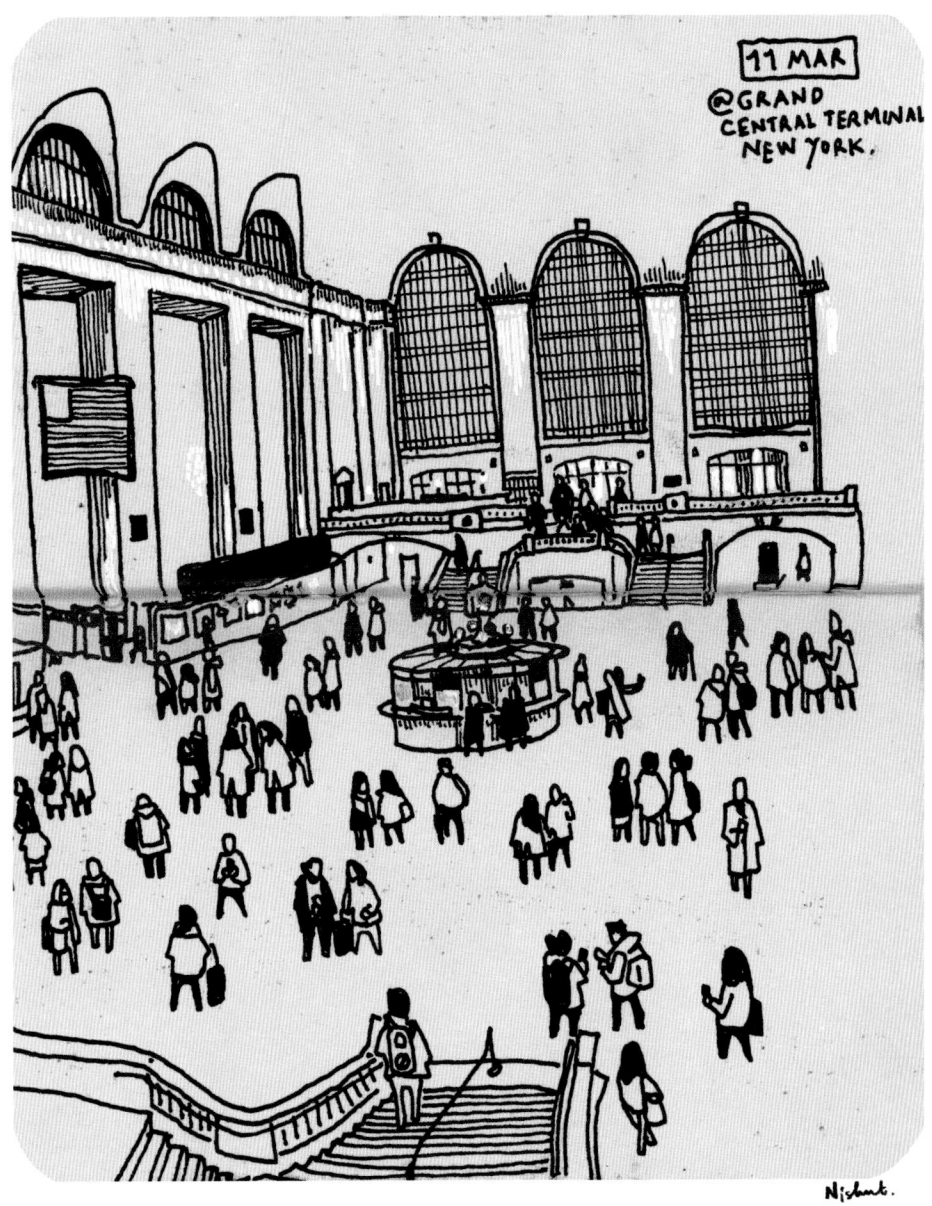

↑  *Observing human activity at Grand Central Terminal, New York City*

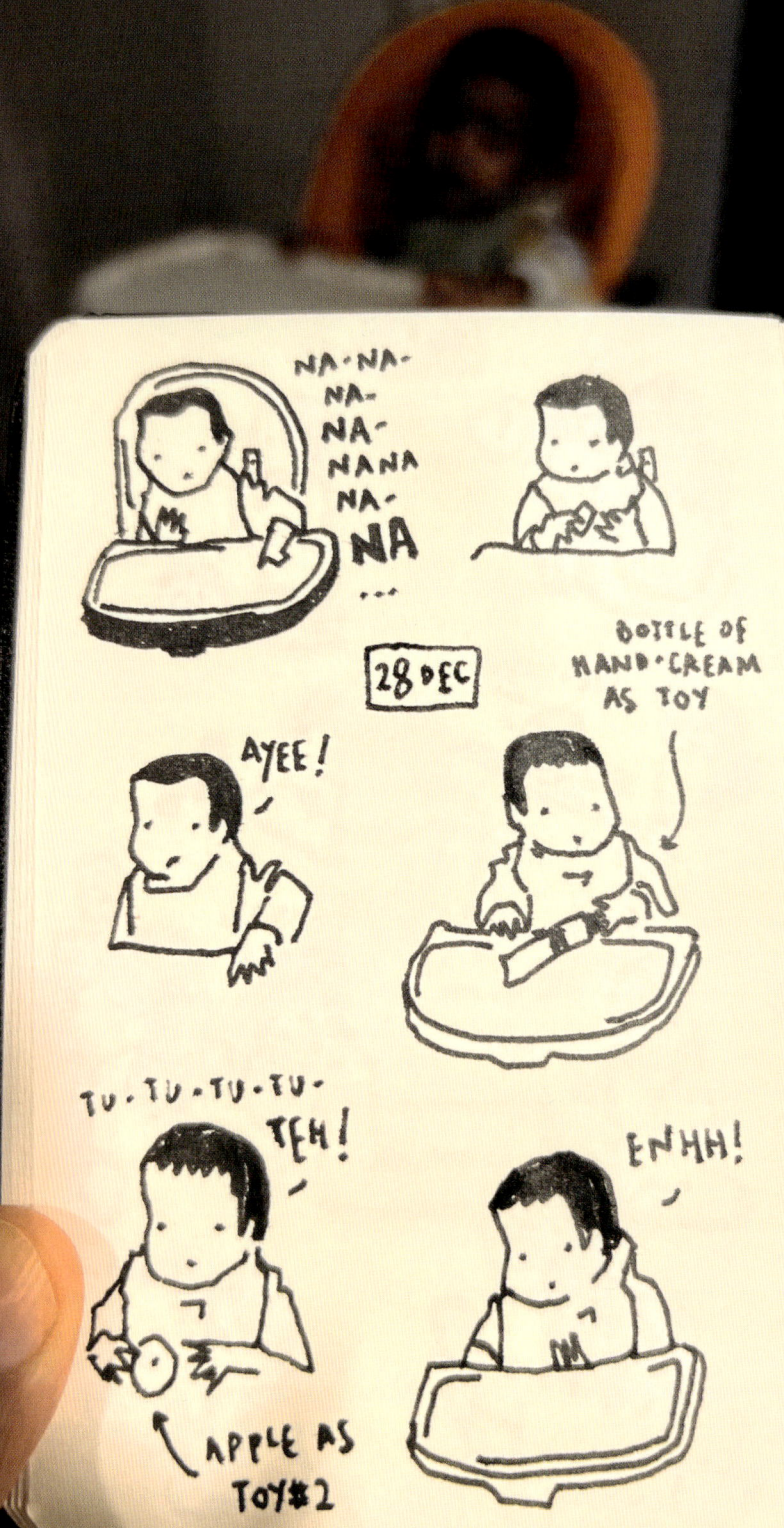

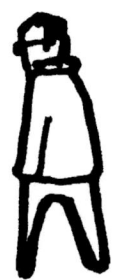

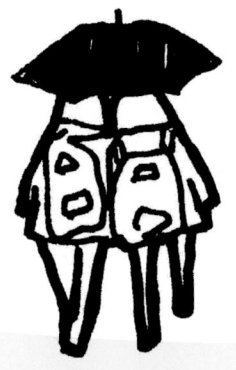

# CHAPTER 8
## MORE GOOD IDEAS: REASONS TO KEEP A SKETCHBOOK

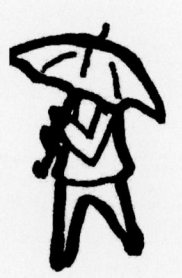

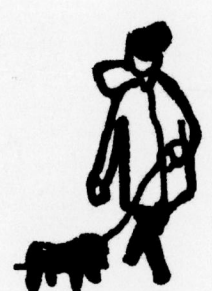

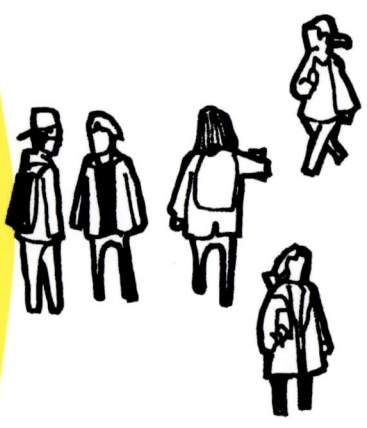

# What is a sketchbook for?

Aren't you tired of *all the words everywhere*? Sometimes I wonder about how quickly we became such a text-heavy society. Messages, emails, summaries, articles, notifications, status updates ... words assault our mind in an endless carousel every single day. But at the same time, it is becoming *more* difficult to explain ourselves to others and to make sense of our world. *Words are terrible at the one thing they are supposed to do— to mean things!*

If you feel the burden of words, a sketchbook is for you. If you have thoughts and ideas you can never find the words for, a sketchbook is for you. If you want to unearth the part of yourself that exists outside of spoken vocabulary, a sketchbook is your best tool.

A sketchbook is a laboratory and a playground. Using line and color, it allows you to play with concepts beyond words and language. It allows you to relate with other people and the world you share with them, without the messy business of adjectives and nouns and verbs. If you let it, a sketchbook can become a visual journal of your life, without a single word getting in the way.

All this is to say that sketchbooks are not just for artists. In fact, even art is not just for artists! It is a peculiarity of modern thought that we separate art and artists from general society. The idea that we can only draw or paint if we are *good enough* is harmful and makes us lesser humans. It is not different from saying that someone should not sing without formal training, or dance at a friend's wedding, or invent stories to put their children to sleep.

Art is the business of all humans everywhere. It helps us say things we could not otherwise say. It gives us a channel of self-expression we could never access anywhere else. It predates written and spoken language. It is in the doodles we make during an idle hour, in the songs we sing, the jokes we crack, the clothes we wear, and in many other subconscious aspects of our self-expression.

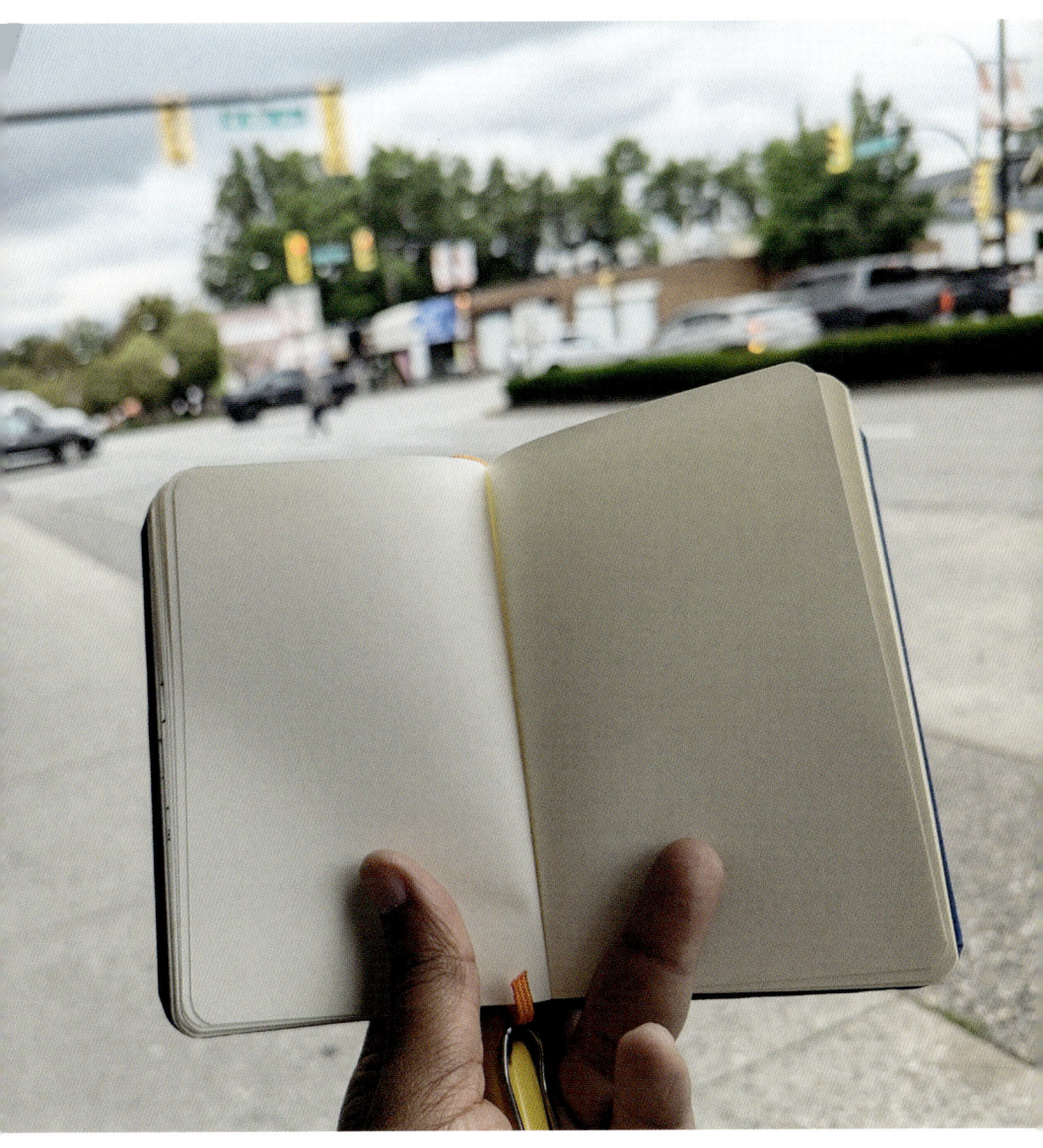

So drawing is a useful habit, regardless of how good you are at it. And in this chapter, I share some good reasons to keep a sketchbook habit.

↑ *A blank sketchbook page is an invitation to sketch.*

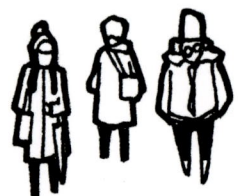

# What Is the Best Sketchbook?

I am asked this question too often. It surprises me because it is one of the least important questions. And it has a very simple answer.

The best sketchbook is the one you are unafraid to use.

If you do not want to "ruin" expensive paper, take a cheap sketchbook and cheap materials to make lots of cheap art. By cheap art, I do not mean art that has less value. I mean art that does not invoke a high monetary cost *from you*. Because anything that lowers the mental cost of starting a drawing is a good thing!

**SNEAKY ART TIP #103**

Every time I finish one sketchbook, I buy a completely different sketchbook—different brand, but also different size. I do this because the sketchbook page is really a frame *through which* you see your world, inside which you compose your scenes. Changing the dimensions is a way to refresh what you see.

For example, drawing a location on a horizontal page and then drawing again with a vertical page leads to significant changes in composition, and ideas represented on the page.

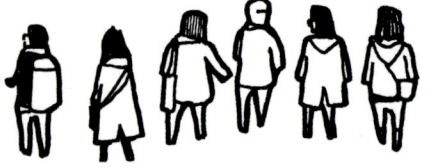

Start the journey quickly, dear reader, because there is a big world of art supplies, papers, and materials to explore!

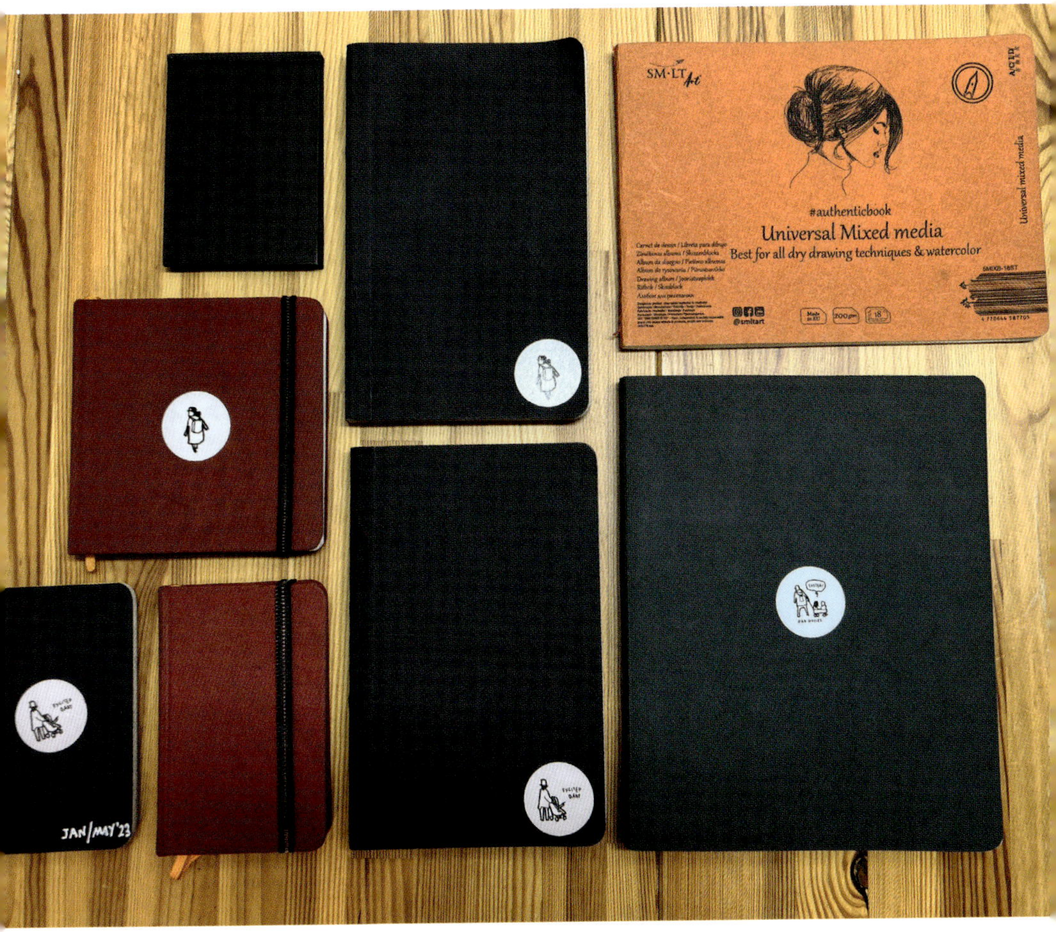

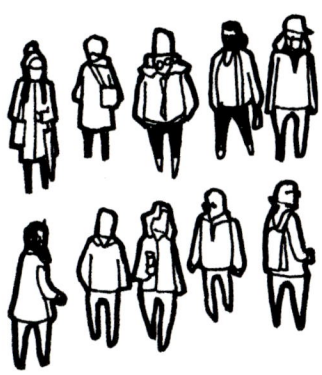

↑ *Some recent sketchbooks I have used*

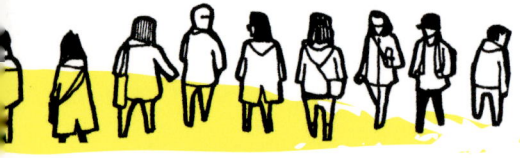

## An Invitation to Spend Time

Soon after I started sketching in Chicago, we moved to a town in the middle of the American Midwest. From a diverse, metropolitan city of the world, I suddenly found myself in a place where no one looked like me. I wanted to keep up my drawing habit, but every time I went out to draw, the same intrusive thoughts ran through my mind: *Am I allowed to occupy this space? How will I blend in?*

At that time, the sketchbook became a crutch for me to lean on. It answered all my hesitations. Yes, I *can* sit alone at the café—I need to make a drawing today. Yes, I *can* go to the farmer's market where no one else looks like me—I need to practice drawing people. Yes, I *can* occupy this seat for another hour—I am learning to use watercolors.

If you, like me, are self-conscious or socially anxious, a sketchbook can be your permission slip. If hesitations plague your mind, putting pen to paper will plug that flow of second thoughts. Because the sketchbook is an invitation to spend time in an unfamiliar space and observe deeply.

My sketchbooks from Eau Claire (Wisconsin) record a journey of exploration and discovery. I learned that differences between people are easy to see because they are at the surface. The deeper you go, the more similar we are to one another. I learned that beauty is not exclusive to big cities. Often it is hidden in plain sight, in ordinary places, at ordinary times of ordinary days, just waiting to be found.

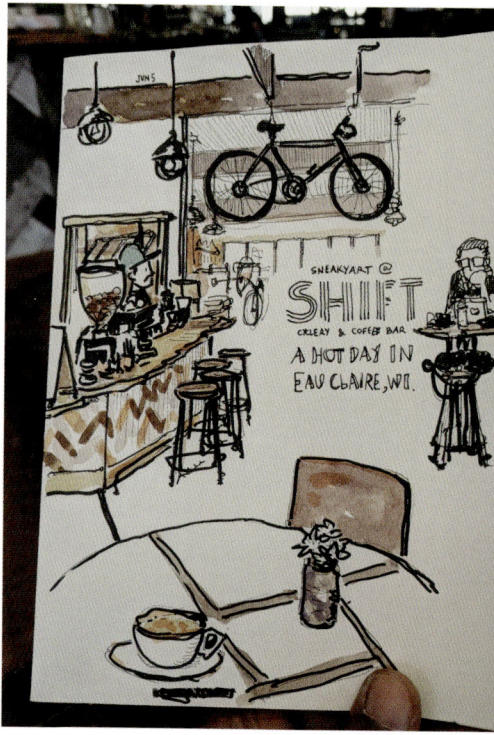

↑  *One of my first times sketching at the Shift Cyclery & Coffee Bar in Eau Claire, Wisconsin, I used watercolors to ensure I spent more time there than for a quick, sneaky sketch.*

# The Gift of Attention

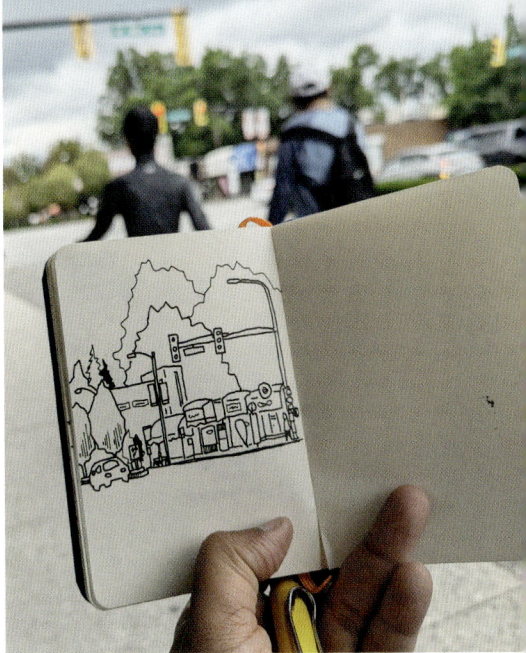

↑  *Quickly, before the bus arrives!*

The Greek philosopher Aristotle considered attention to be the vehicle of time—that the passage of time is felt only by our observation of change. When we do not actively notice things, such as when driving home along a familiar route, time flies by. When we observe deeply, such as when walking the streets of a foreign city, time passes more slowly. By paying active attention to our environment, we control the passage of time.

In busy times, therefore, it is crucial that we be able to control our attention. Unfortunately, the richest corporations and CEOs of the world are busy devising technologies to most effectively capture and monetize it. Every page on every website, every app on your phone, every company everywhere, wants a portion of your attention. Cut and sliced, ripped and shattered, we are left with only fragments and torn pieces of our active, curious, thinking mind. *A sketchbook is a tool to reclaim your attention span and enrich your time.*

Sitting with just the blank page and your world before you, a sketchbook habit invites you to indulge your curiosity. It empowers you to direct your attention toward the things you enjoy, instead of doing free labor for manipulative algorithms and corporate marketing budgets.

A sketchbook is the gift of attention you give yourself.

Shown here: While waiting for the bus, I opened my little pad to draw this scene. I thought about the large trees in my part of the world, and how they tower over the urban ecosystem. It was a simple thought, an idle curiosity, and I was able to indulge it in the few minutes before my bus arrived.

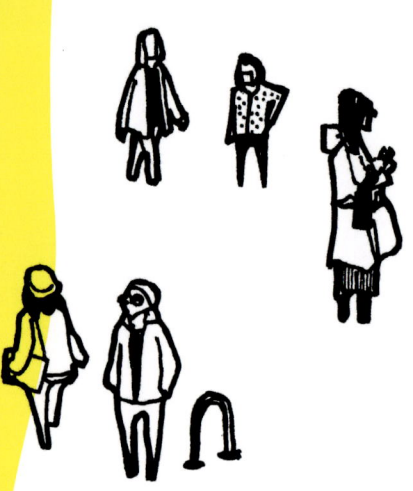

## Room for Magic

When I go out to draw, I do not know what I will find. But after filling up many sketchbooks, I know to trust the process. My job is simply to see the world with curious eyes. When I see something, I give it my time and attention. **Every drawing begins this way, with the implicit trust that something magical is right around the corner.**

A sketchbook reinforces the lesson that magic can still be found. Sometimes it appears in the smallest things, and sometimes those are the most beautiful. **All you have to do is leave room for it—on your page, in your day, and in your life.**

At first, this was not easy for me. All of us suffer from the terrible malady of adulthood, i.e., rejecting magical unknowns for something predictable. To be an adult means not doing things unless you are sure of what you will get, i.e., a solid ROI (Return on Investment). So as we get older, we do fewer new things and make fewer discoveries and our world becomes smaller and our minds become narrower as a result.

When we first arrived in Vancouver, I saw a woman walk into the park on a cold and rainy morning with a grocery bag. Wondering what she was up to, I pulled out my sketchbook. I started drawing just as she pulled out a loaf of bread, tore chunks, and threw them into the air. Then I heard the crows. Dozens of birds swirled in the air around her— crows, pigeons, and seagulls too—and she had enough bread for everyone. The next morning, when I heard the birds again, I saw that she had arrived. She was there every morning, regardless of weather. And it felt like I belonged to a magical, beautiful world, because I was sharing it with her.

→  *A woman feeding birds in the park*

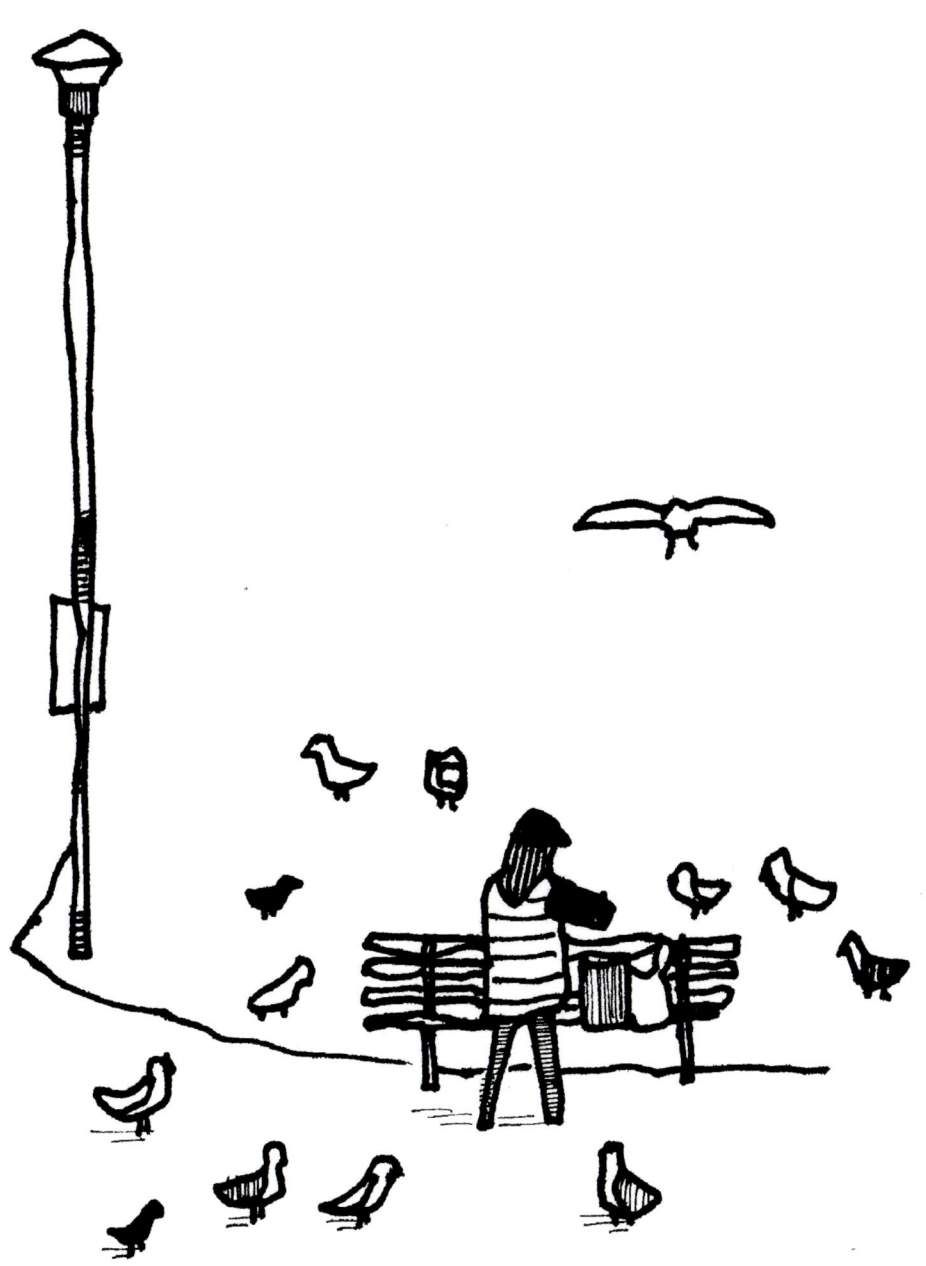

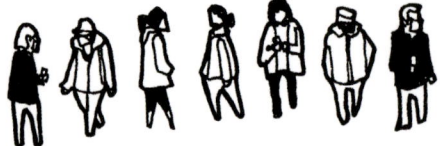 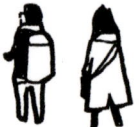 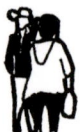

# A Chance to Discover Yourself

When you draw from observation, your eyes observe the world, and your hands translate that on the page. But inside this equation, the information passes through several other filters of your mind: *How do you feel about what you see? Where do your eyes linger? What do they gloss over? What shapes do you enjoy? Which colors excite you?* Beyond the biological filter of eyesight lie the filters that determine how you see what you see. These filters constitute your taste, your preferences, your personality.

A sketchbook habit led by curiosity can teach you many things about your outside world. At the same time, it can teach you many things about yourself.

I already knew I was an impatient person, but one of the first things I learned from drawing in beautiful Chicago was that I had zero patience for all the skyscrapers with their windows! My eyes were drawn to the human activity at ground level, and buildings simply played the role of backdrop to this urban action.

It can be difficult when you begin, because we are so used to devaluing our curiosity. But if you allow it to lead the way, the sketchbook page will tell you who you are.

→ *The first drawing someone bought from me*

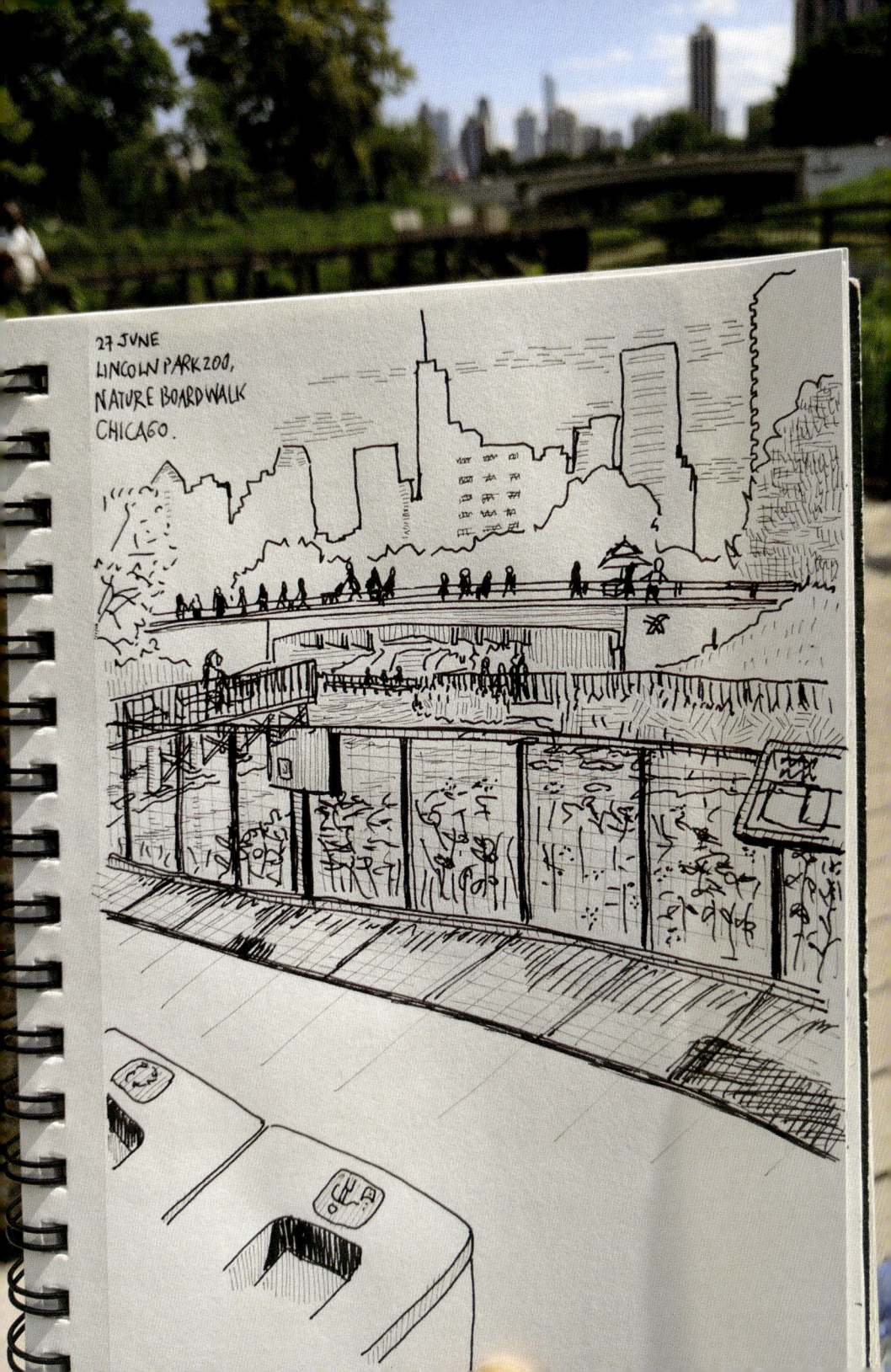

27 JUNE
LINCOLN PARK ZOO,
NATURE BOARDWALK
CHICAGO.

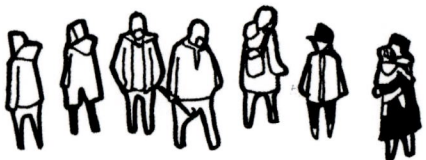

# A Record of a Changing World

When my son was born, I started a practice of drawing him every day. As of this writing, he is less than a year old, but I already have multiple sketchbooks of little Rohan. Early parenthood can be a rough journey, and the interrupted sleep patterns can mess with your sense of time and memory. Without the benefit of my sketchbook pages, I would not remember the thousands of little things Rohan did, the things he learned, and the different ways he grew from week to week and month to month.

Shown here, a moment of bonding between Rohan and his grandparents. And, at six months, I was ready with my sketchbook when Rohan woke from a nap and rolled over for the first time!

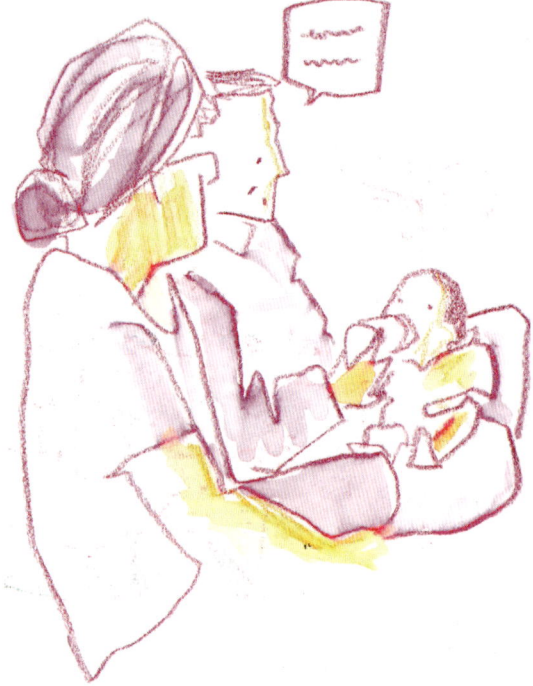

↑ *Rohan with his grandparents*

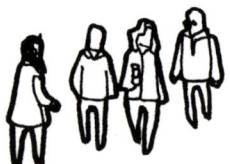

→ *The first time Rohan rolled over!*

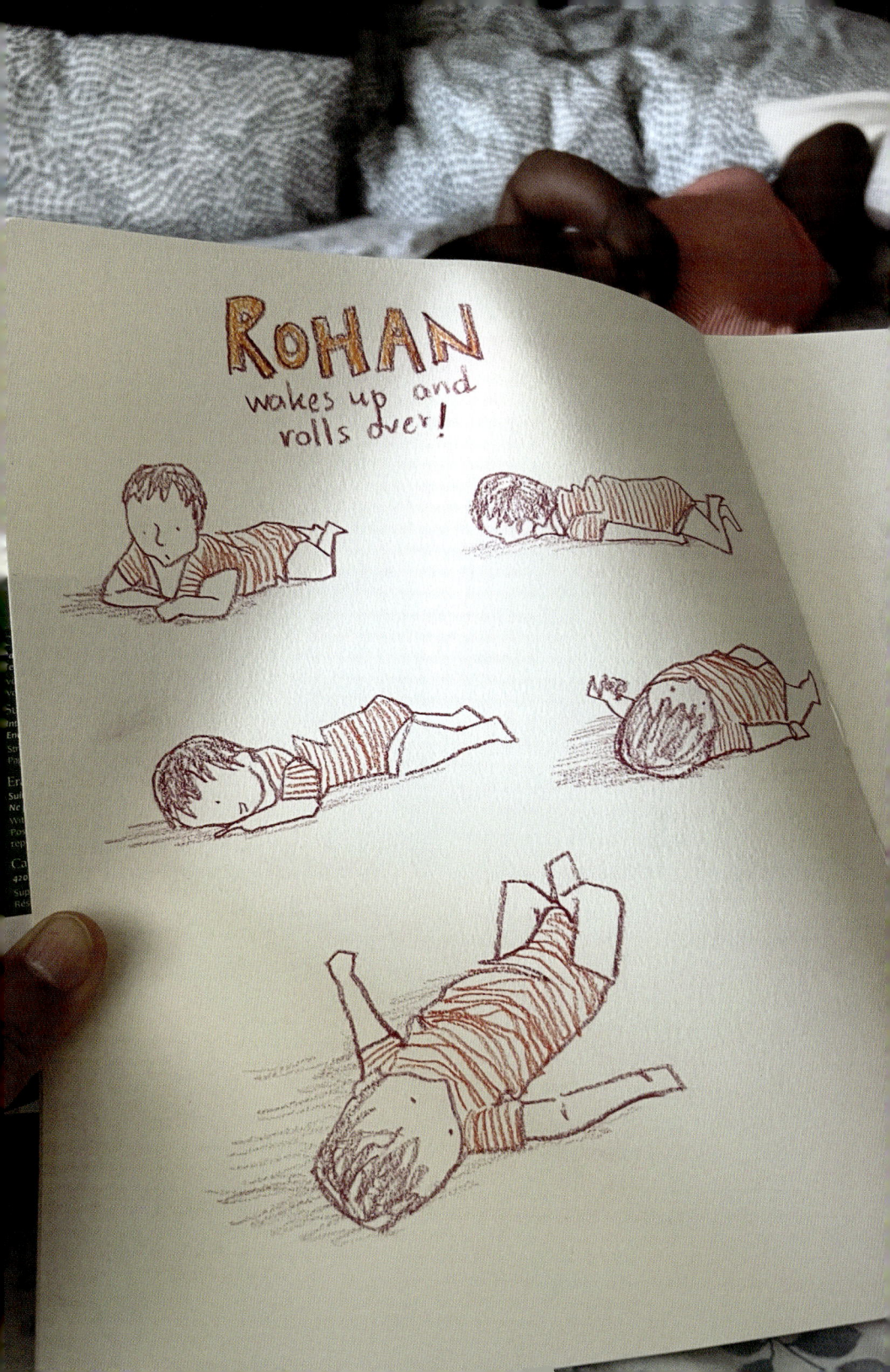

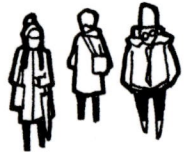

# A Way to Remember Everything

I open an old sketchbook to a random page from months or even years ago and I see more than just those lines that I drew. As if trapped within the pages, countless other memories unlock in my mind.

Memory is constructed out of sensory stimuli. It's what you hear and what you see, but also what you smell and touch. Sensory stimuli includes the feeling of the wind on your arm, the sharp edge of a stone under your seat, and the innumerable, unvoiced emotions, thoughts, and feelings that ran through your mind on a particular day. We do not consciously make these memories, but the mind finds a place for them, in an attic somewhere, dormant until they are triggered.

Turning the page to October in Chicago, I can feel the autumn winds, and the jacket I wore to protect myself. Turning to February in Vancouver, I can taste the hot coffee in the warm interior of the café, and hear the buzz of conversations in the air. On some pages I can tell which podcast or song I was listening to. My attention was on my subjects, and on the business of translating reality to my page, but meanwhile my mind was collecting and storing all kinds of information.

Shown: At the seawall in Vancouver, I remember the cold wind coming in off the ocean, and my fingers starting to freeze. It started to rain when I was halfway through the sketch. I tried to shield the page, but not before one fat drop of water fell on it. Can you see it?

→ *Rained upon, at the seawall*

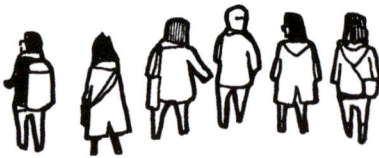

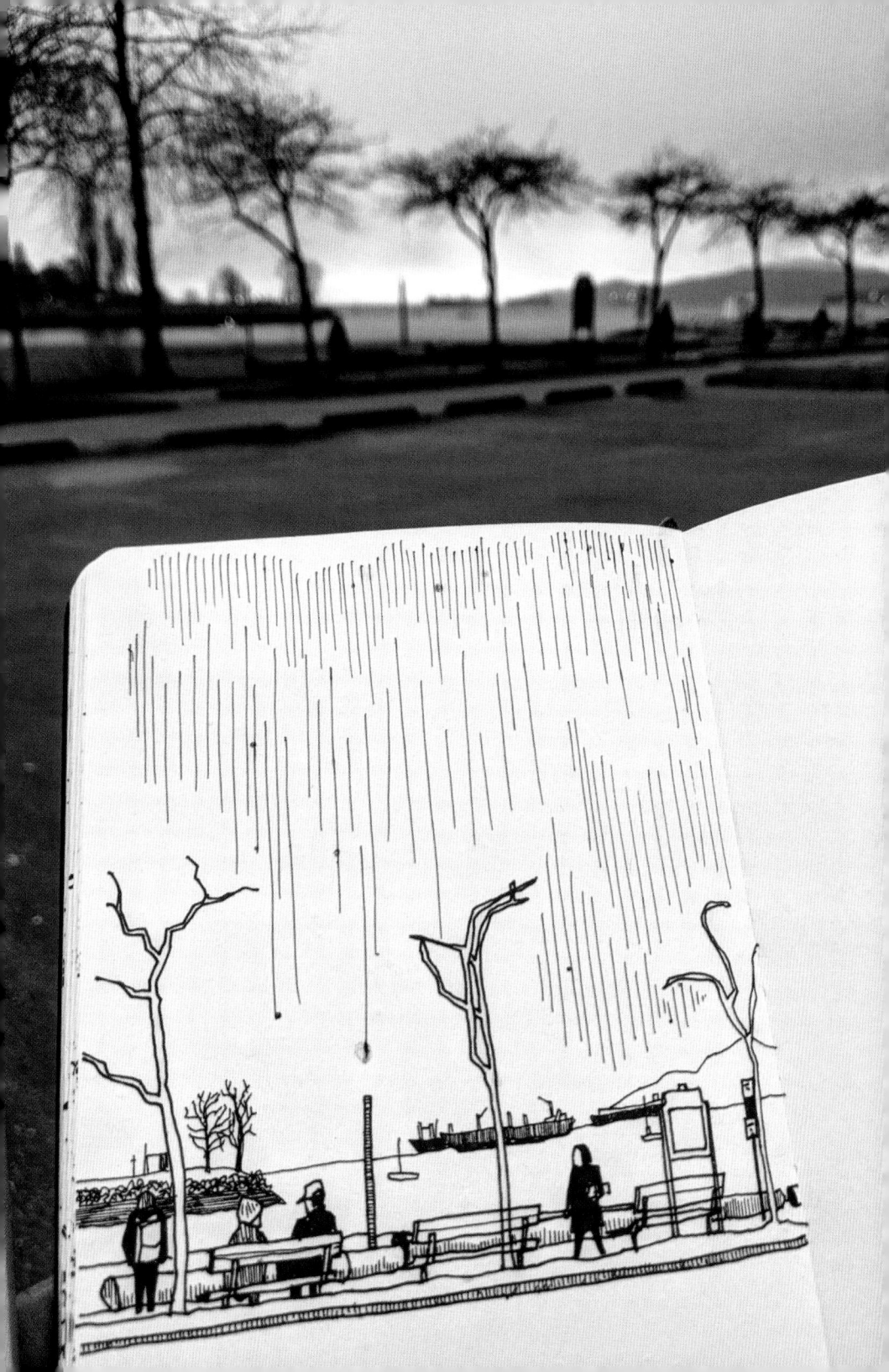

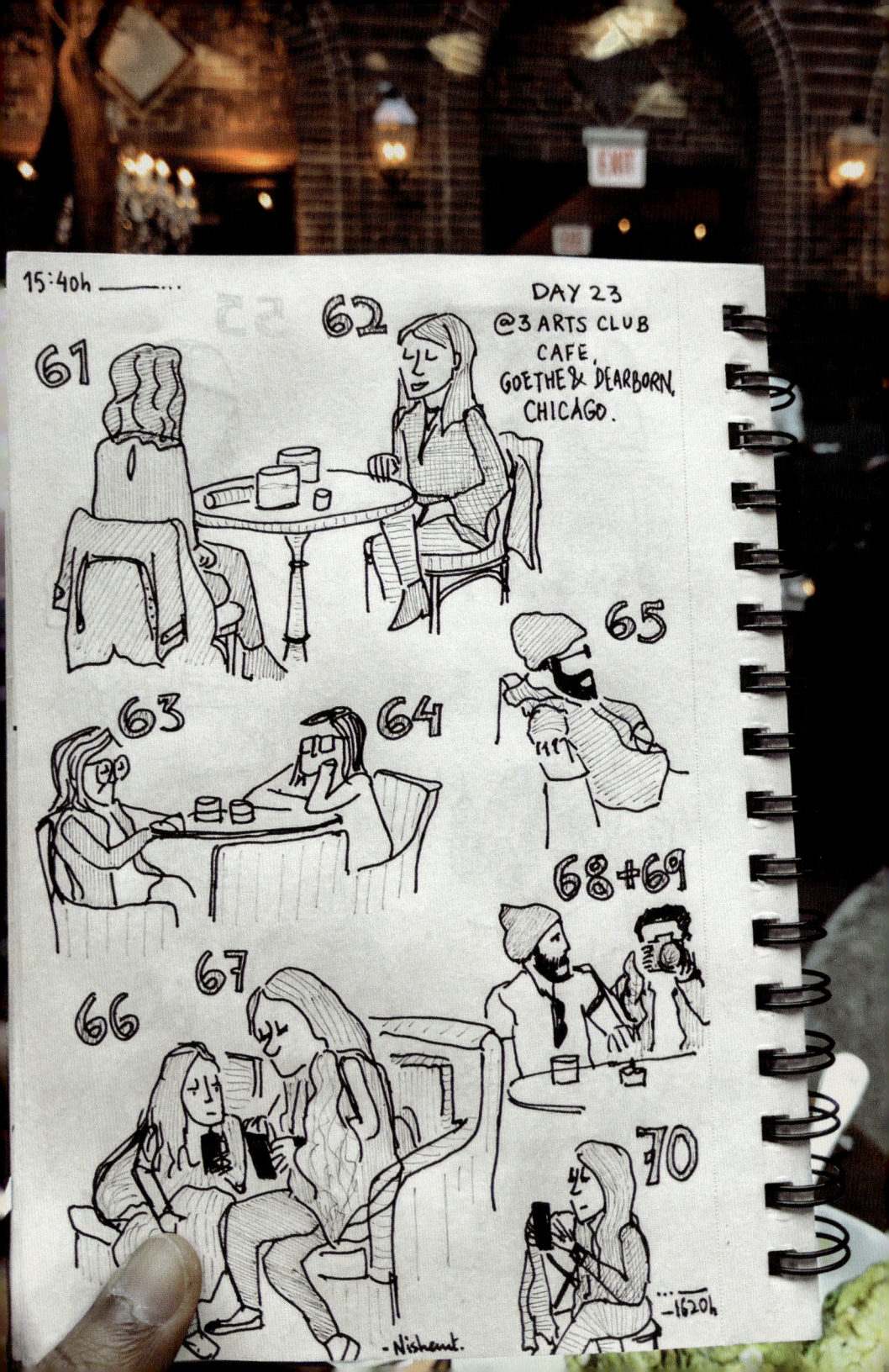

15:40h ——— ...

DAY 23
@ 3 ARTS CLUB
CAFE,
GOETHE & DEARBORN,
CHICAGO.

61

62

63

64

65

66

67

68+69

70

—Nishant.

...—1620h

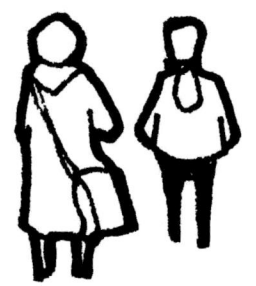

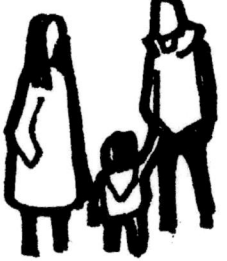

# CHAPTER 9
## VISUAL DIARY:
## BUILD A SKETCHBOOK HABIT

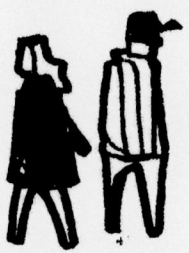

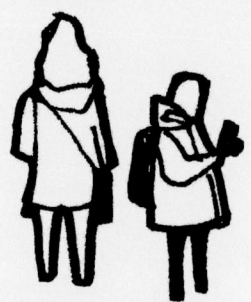

# Find a Community:
## The #OneWeek100People Challenge

I learned about the #OneWeek100People challenge when I was grappling with drawing people myself. It takes place annually every second week of March, and I joined the Facebook group a little before, to follow daily posts from thousands of people around the world.

You can do a OneWeek100People challenge by yourself, anytime you like. But being part of a community is a special little thing that gives you encouragement, fresh ideas, and the beautiful understanding that art has many aspects, that any approach can be valid, that each of us is on our own path of exploration. It shows us that we are not alone in the obstacles we face.

You can tackle the five-day week as a twenty-portraits-per-day challenge. Or you could mix it up: silhouettes one day, and portraits the next. You could do every session as an hour at a café, giving yourself less than three minutes per subject. Or, to really give up the illusion of control, you could do one-minute sketches for only twenty minutes per day. Quick sketching like that leaves you no time to be perfect, and many people

find that to be liberating! In the group, I found people drawing from pictures, and sometimes sticking with specific themes like favorite actors, sportspersons, or leaders. We have our different motivations, and the larger goal of one hundred people invites us to use whatever works for us.

The idea is that, while your initial work may not please you, the week-long goal of 100 people will help you make a lot of progress in relatively little time.

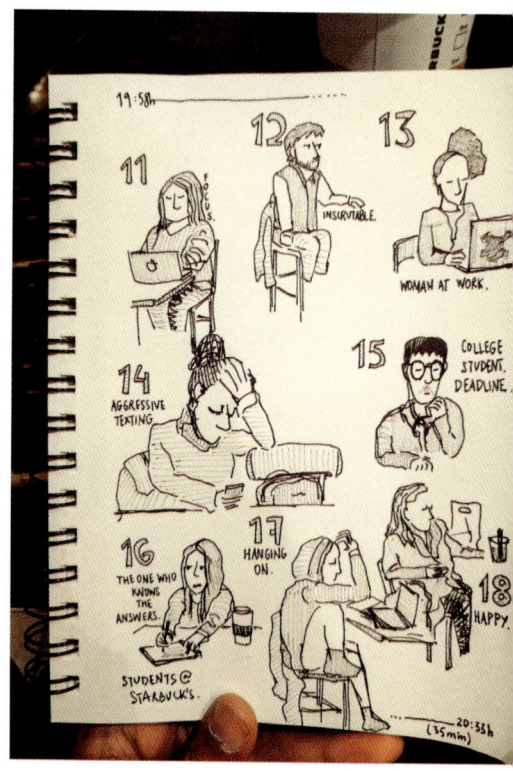

↑  *I put myself on a time deadline too, just for kicks.*

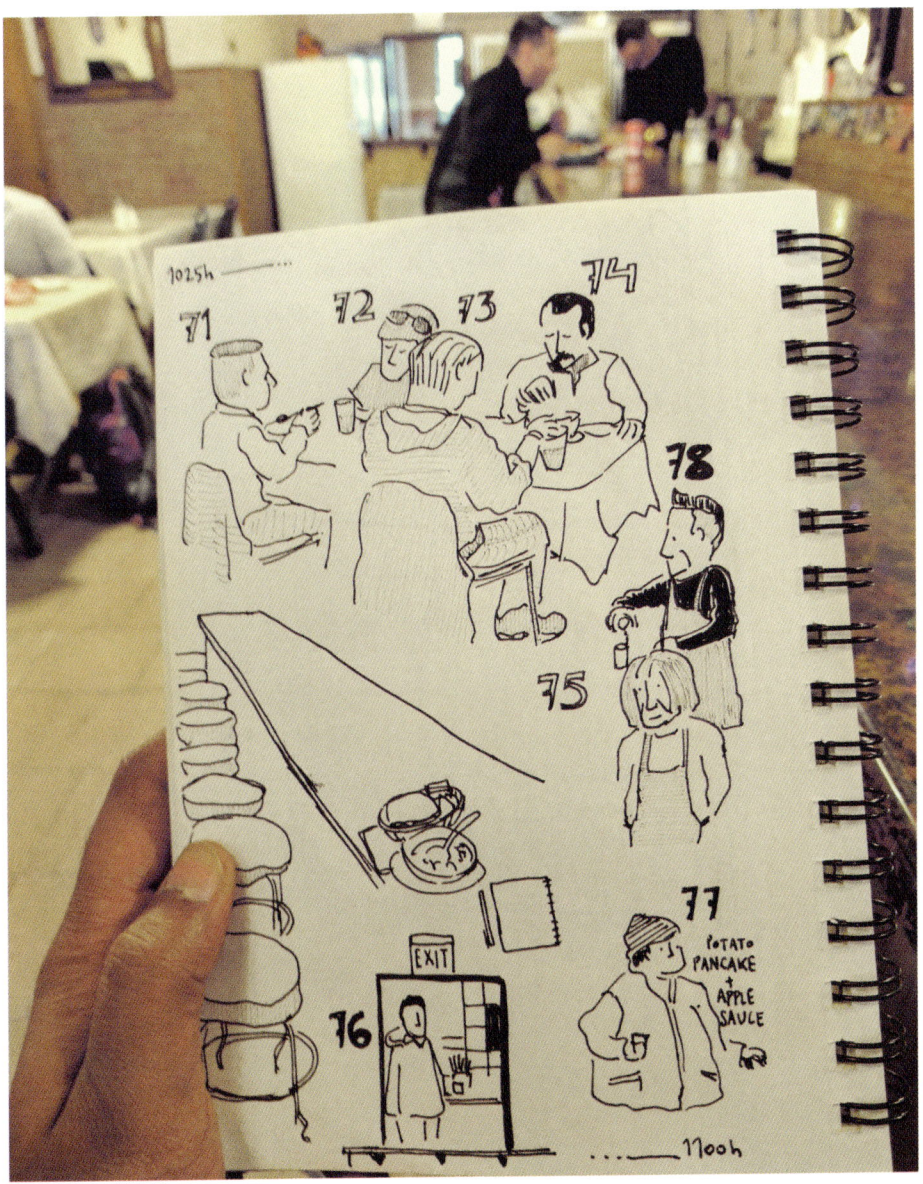

↑ *Drawing different people became an
excuse to visit different neighborhoods.*

# Make Time from Nothing: The Five-Minute Habit

For many people, finding time to draw is difficult. Schedules are busy and chaotic. Energy levels fluctuate throughout the day. But a drawing habit should require neither a huge investment of time nor energy. Sometimes it is as simple as carrying a little sketchbook in your pocket and grabbing a five-minute opportunity to draw.

A five-minute sketch is a beautiful thing. It is not enough time for a detailed drawing, but it is enough for a quick scribble. It is not enough time to work on a large sheet of paper, but it is enough for a little sketch pad that fits in the palm of your hand. It is not enough time to get everything right, but it can be just enough to get one thing right, that one thing that made you want to draw, that one thing that caught your eye.

A five-minute drawing practice may not be enough time to become an artist, but it can be oddly empowering. Day after day, page after page, it shows us how much we can accomplish when we make time to observe our world.

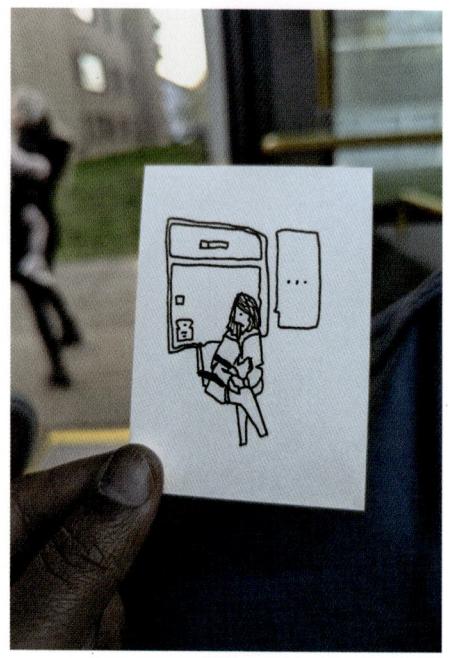

↑ *A five-minute sketch of a co-passenger on the bus ride home*

→ *A quick sketch to think about the other people we encounter in transit*

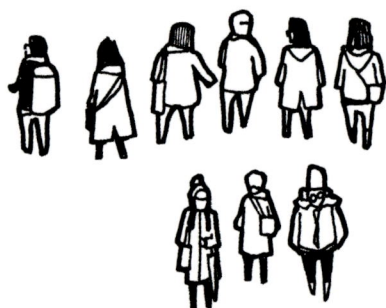

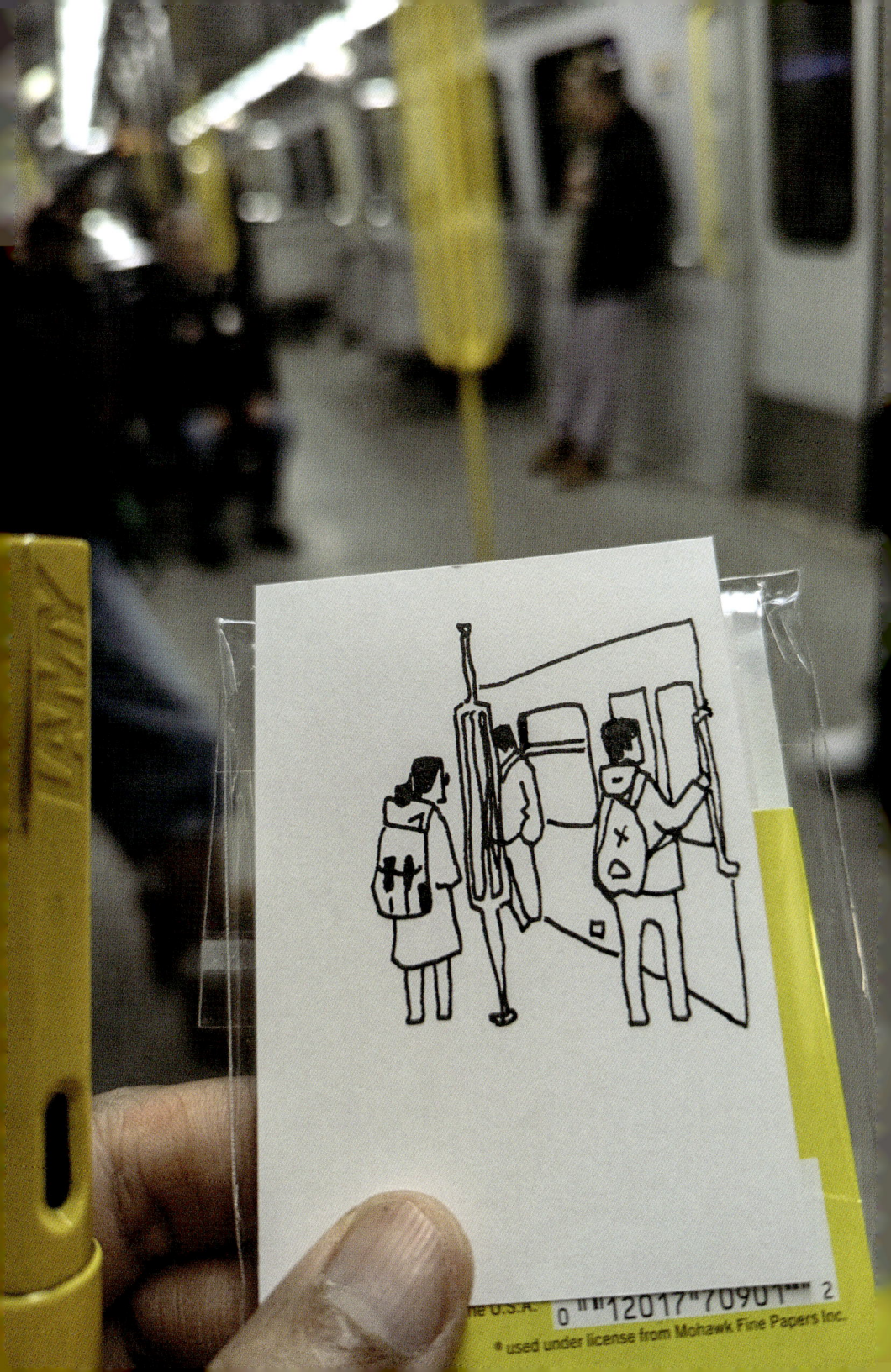

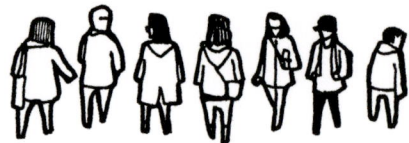

## Keep It Fresh: Look for the New

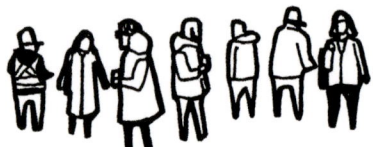

For those of us who suffer from decision anxiety, a clear rule to draw can make things a lot simpler. For those of us easily bored, looking for new things can be exciting. A drawing habit can function this way, supporting and taking advantage of our distracted minds. (Can you tell I am talking about myself?)

Make it your business to notice what is new in your environment. Notice what you have not drawn before, whether it is some lines or the shapes they form or the way two colors sit next to each other. Imagine you are adding those lines, shapes, and colors to a library inside your mind. Imagine every page helping you expand your library of good lines, good shapes, and good colors. So the next time you go out to draw, you know one thing more than you did yesterday.

→ *I do not draw birds often, but they were so still, it felt like an invitation to try a new thing.*

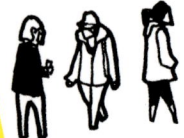

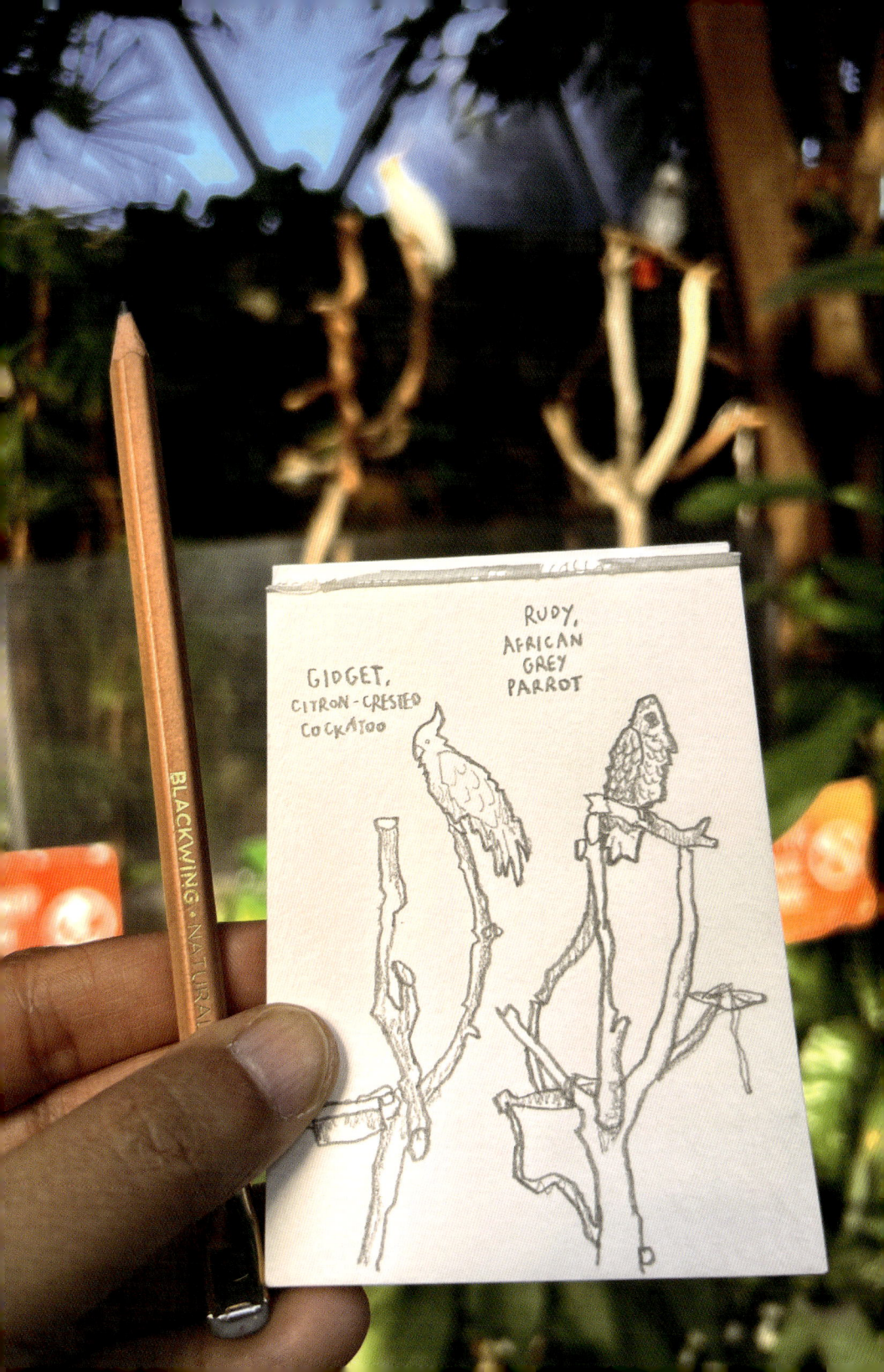

# Keep It Challenging: Change Sketchbooks!

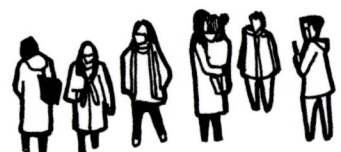

I am a big proponent of changing your sketchbook style as soon as you finish one. Change the size, change the format, change the brand, change the paper type!

Every sketchbook is a frame through which you see the world. The size of the page determines how detailed your drawings can be. The format decides the composition of elements. The paper type affects what tools you use, and how your marks look. And there are so many wonderful brands, big and small, that loyalty to any one is a disservice to your journey of discovery and exploration.

**SNEAKY ART TIP #129**

To ease into color, use a toned-paper sketchbook. Let the toned-paper be the first color of your sketch. Now you just have to add the second . . . and the third!

→ *A gray-toned sketchbook for gray days of winter in Vancouver and the chance to capture Taylor Swift mania*

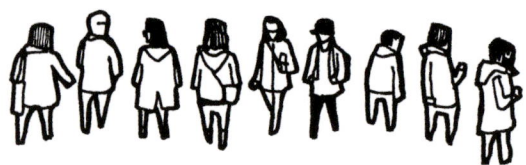

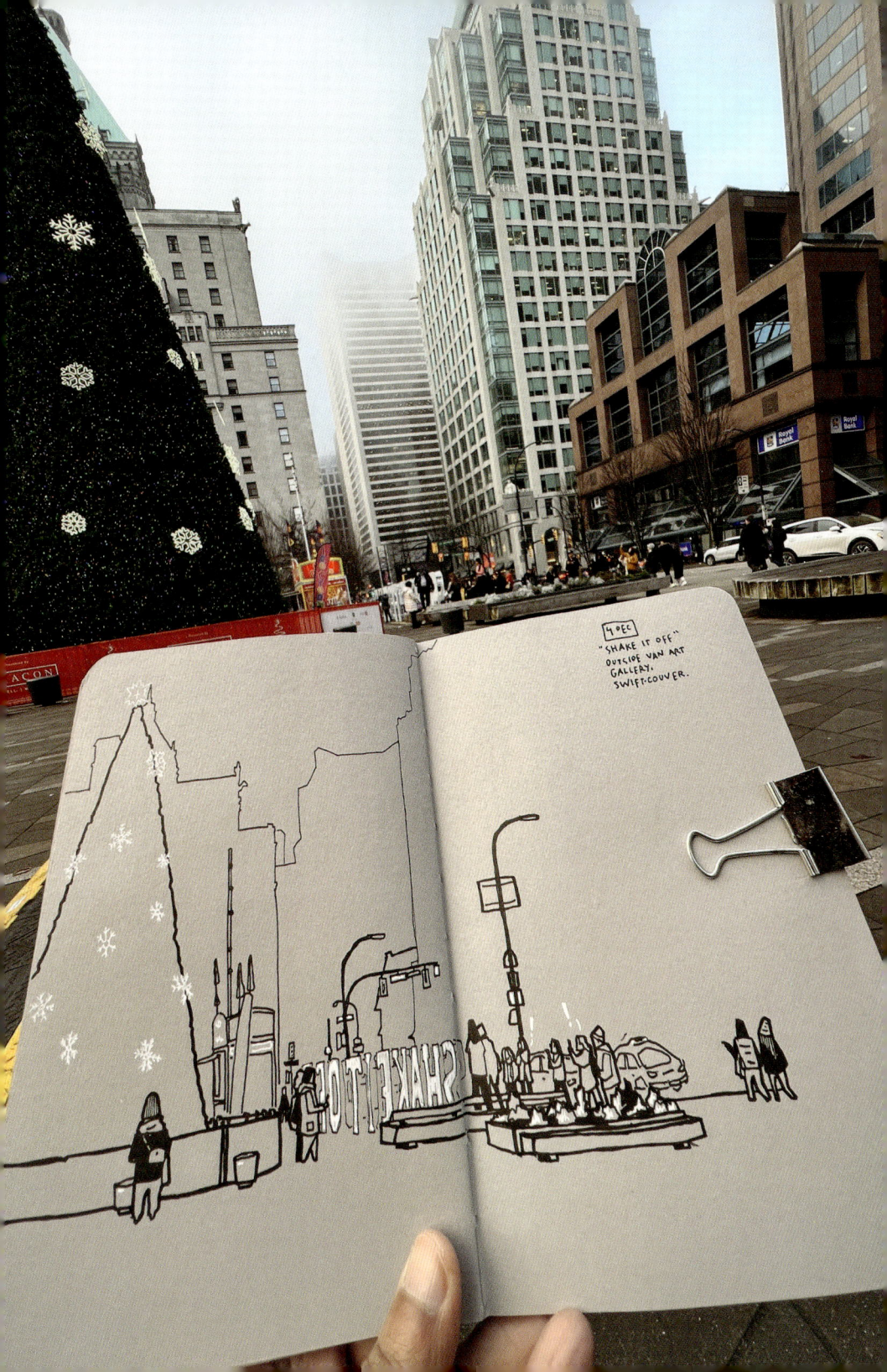

4 DEC
"SHAKE IT OFF"
OUTSIDE VAN ART
GALLERY,
SWIFT·COUVER.

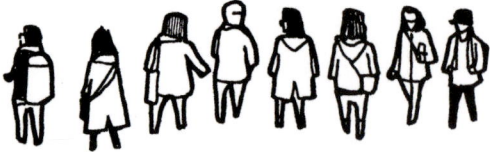

# Keep It Real:
# The secret sketchbook

In his book *Psychopolitics*, philosopher Byung-chul Han explains the curious phenomenon created by the presence of social media in our lives. He describes it as a panopticon—an environment in which everyone feels constantly monitored and judged by everyone else. A social panopticon inhibits our freedom and self-expression by subtly dictating what we allow ourselves to do, with the looming threat of social judgment from our peers. It is a prison without any guards, in which the inmates curtail each other's freedom!

I bring this up because social media also exposes us to the art practices of people around the world. We see their beautiful work, we measure the like counts, we read the positive comments under their posts, and it tells us that we could never be good enough. What is the use of drawing, since it won't be as good as this or that person? Why should I make art if it won't even get a tenth of those likes? The effect of social media is that of a virus that has infiltrated all our minds. Every time we take a photo of the sunset, or look at ourselves in the mirror, or think about drawing on a blank page, it whispers the imagined opinions of other people to discourage us.

Your art is not for other people, if you do not want it to be. Its primary function, always, is to serve you. It is your channel of self-expression, and sometimes it's not for anyone else. It could be a self-expression for yourself. So it is vital that you keep out the voices of other people, the opinions of nameless ghosts, the amalgam of every discouraging thought that tells you to not do a thing because it would not be popular enough or good enough or viral enough.

One of the ways to do this is to keep a secret sketchbook. Share it with no one. Do not even tell others of its existence. Find a tailor in a shady back alley who will stitch a secret pocket in your jacket, a secret pocket for your secret art. Make clandestine drawings from the corner seat of cafés, and chuckle to yourself when you do a good thing. Laugh if it looks silly. Build a space where you allow yourself to express your curiosity, and explore your environment. And remember, the goal is not to make good art or good-enough art or viral or popular things. The goal is to scratch your creative itch, to have that conversation with yourself, to be a sneaky artist.

Let the sketchbook take you on a double journey of discovery: the external journey of the environment around you, and the internal voyage inside your own mind.

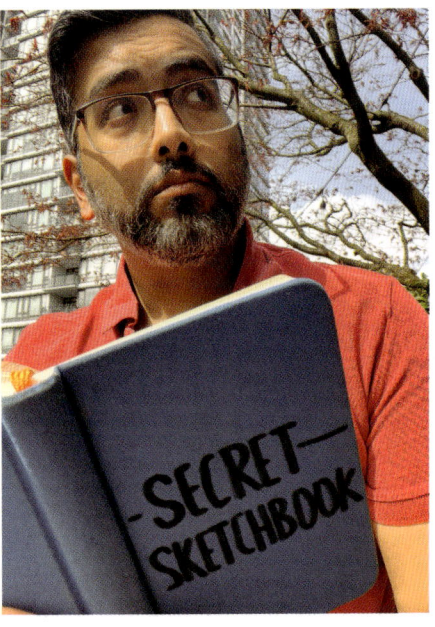

→ *Just casually drawing without raising suspicions*

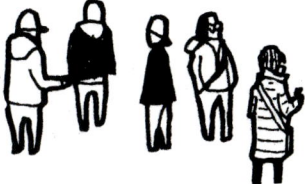

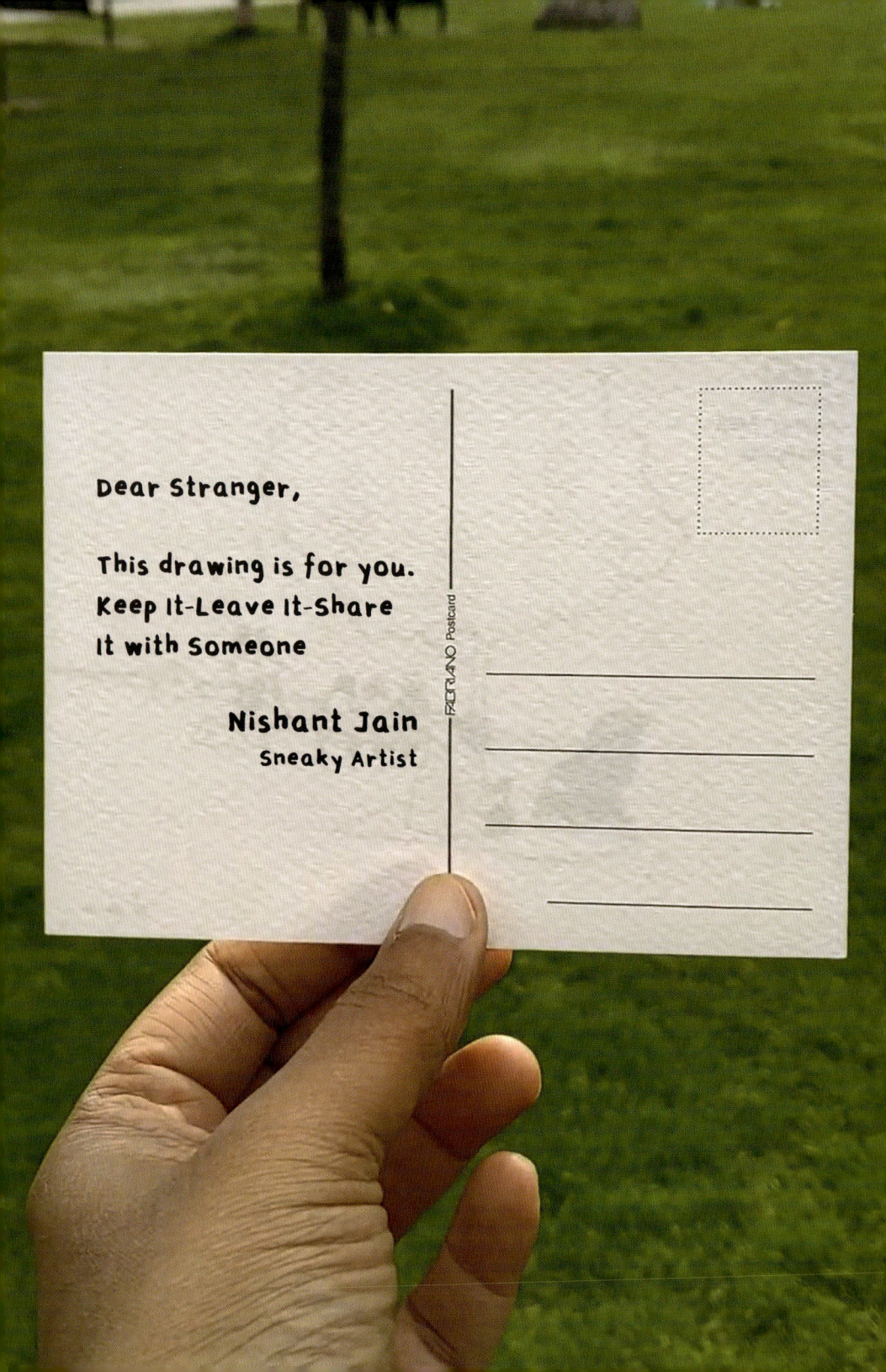

Dear Stranger,

This drawing is for you.
Keep It-Leave It-Share
It with Someone

Nishant Jain
Sneaky Artist

FABRIANO Postcard

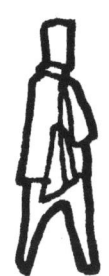

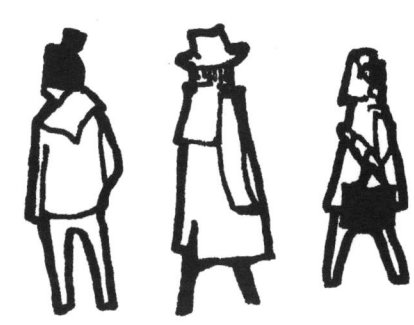

# CHAPTER 10
## WHAT'S NEXT:
## CONCLUDING THOUGHTS

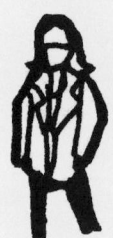

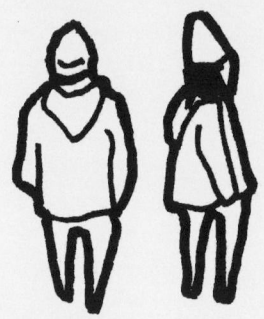

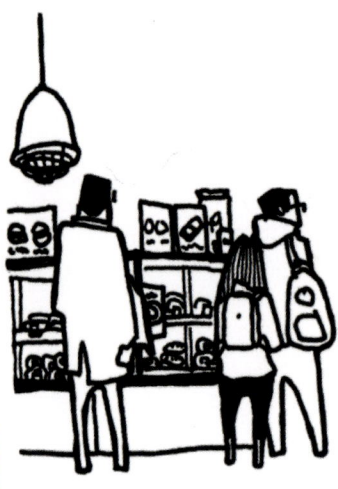

# Be the Curator of Your Own Gallery

I had made hundreds of drawings and been selling art for a couple of years already before I framed a piece to put up on the walls of our home. It was a cheap frame of synthetic wood hanging off a yellow pin above the living room couch, but in the morning sunlight it looked very special indeed. For me, it was a transformative moment. I could not believe I had not done this before. Whose permission had I been waiting for?

Reader, do not wait for permission. Treat your art like it is Art. You made something. Be proud of it.

A decent frame can add luster and dignity to your work. It can give you the opportunity to see your work from a metaphorical *and* literal distance. For me, the first time I looked at my framed drawing,

I realized beauty has little to do with skill or expertise. You can love a thing for just being itself. And that drawing on the wall, separated from the other sketchbook pages, was a beautiful reminder of my journey to become an artist.

### SNEAKY ART TIP #478

Do not stop at framing. Paste a little tag under the piece, telling its little story. Give it a title too. And write "NFS" below that to say: Not For Sale.

→ *Daily drawings of my son, framed on the living room wall*

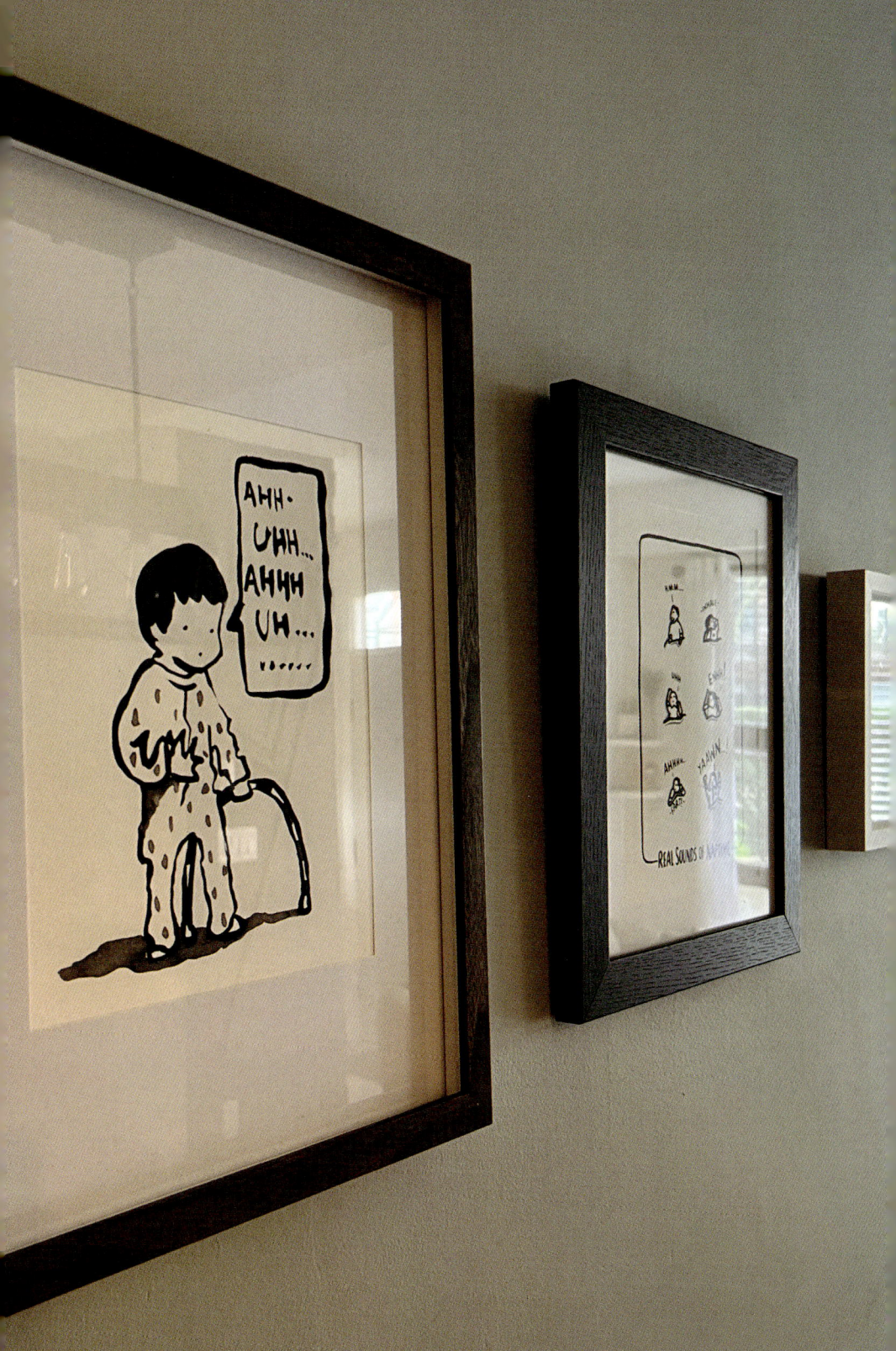

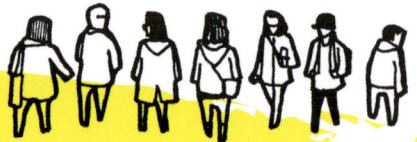

# Give Art to Friends and Family

You know how to draw. But what of it? Can your art play a useful role in your life, and in the lives of people around you?

When wrapping a gift for someone's birthday, insert a quickly sketched portrait too. Your art will have more value than its technical proficiency. It will be a sign that you thought about them enough to make something special just for them.

Make holiday cards out of your drawings. Draw tiny portraits at social gatherings and family get-togethers. Whether it is framed on their walls or kept inside their wallets, whether it sits on a mantelpiece or remains on their phone screens, your art has the ability to make someone's world just a little bit more beautiful. And that right there is a little bit of a superpower.

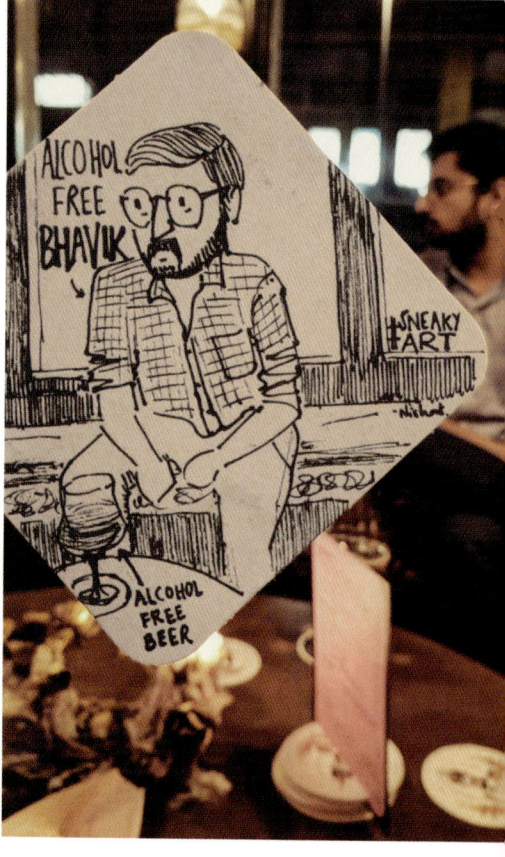

↑ *A drawing on a coaster for a friend*

# Leave Art for Strangers to Find

Vancouver has dozens of Little Free Libraries all over the city—small posts in people's front yards with a shelf full of free books. People are welcome to take any book they like, or leave any book they wish to give away. I love these libraries because they inculcate a generous atmosphere of sharing and community-building. So every time I find one, I leave a tiny drawing in there, hidden inside one of the books. I think of it as a surprise for the wonderful people who take or contribute books to these free libraries.

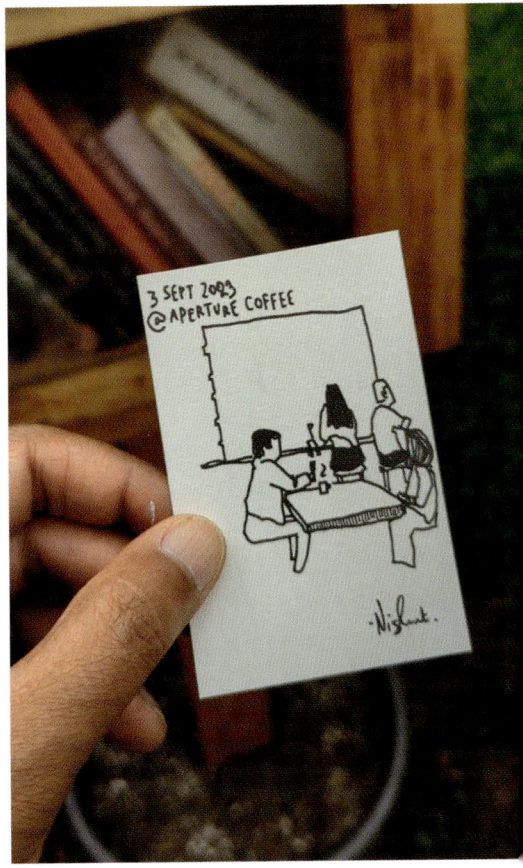

↑ *A little drawing left inside a Little Free Library in Vancouver*

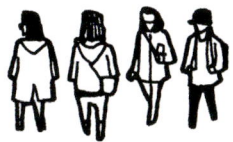

# Join a Local Art Group

There is nothing better than finding people who are obsessed with the same things as you. Whether it is a love of sketchbooks or pencils or inks or color, joining a local art group will let you share your enthusiasm with other like-minded people. When I learned about the practice of urban sketching, I was lucky to also find an active chapter in the city where I lived. Joining the biweekly meetups had a tremendous impact on my art, helped me make friends in a new part of the world, and became an important outlet for my creativity.

The only downside is that art supplies are a dangerous rabbit hole, and you may find yourself spending far more than you intended on a fourth or fifth (or sixth!) bottle of ink. Tread carefully.

→ *A sketchbook throwdown at an Urban Sketchers meetup in Chicago*

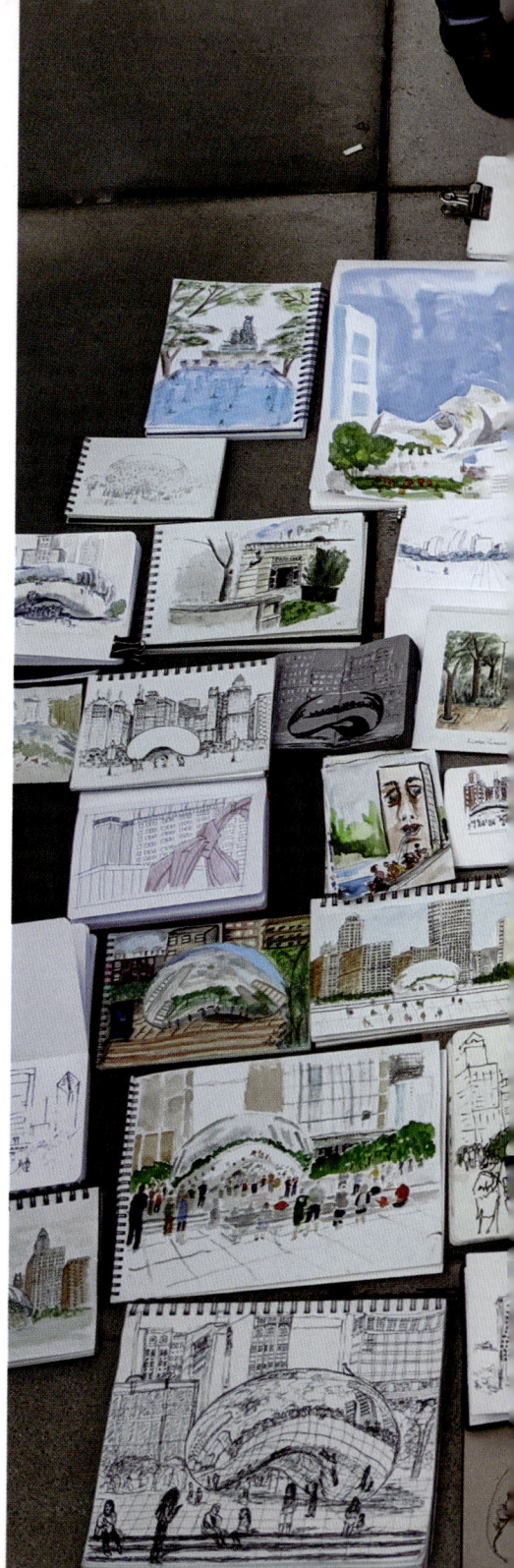

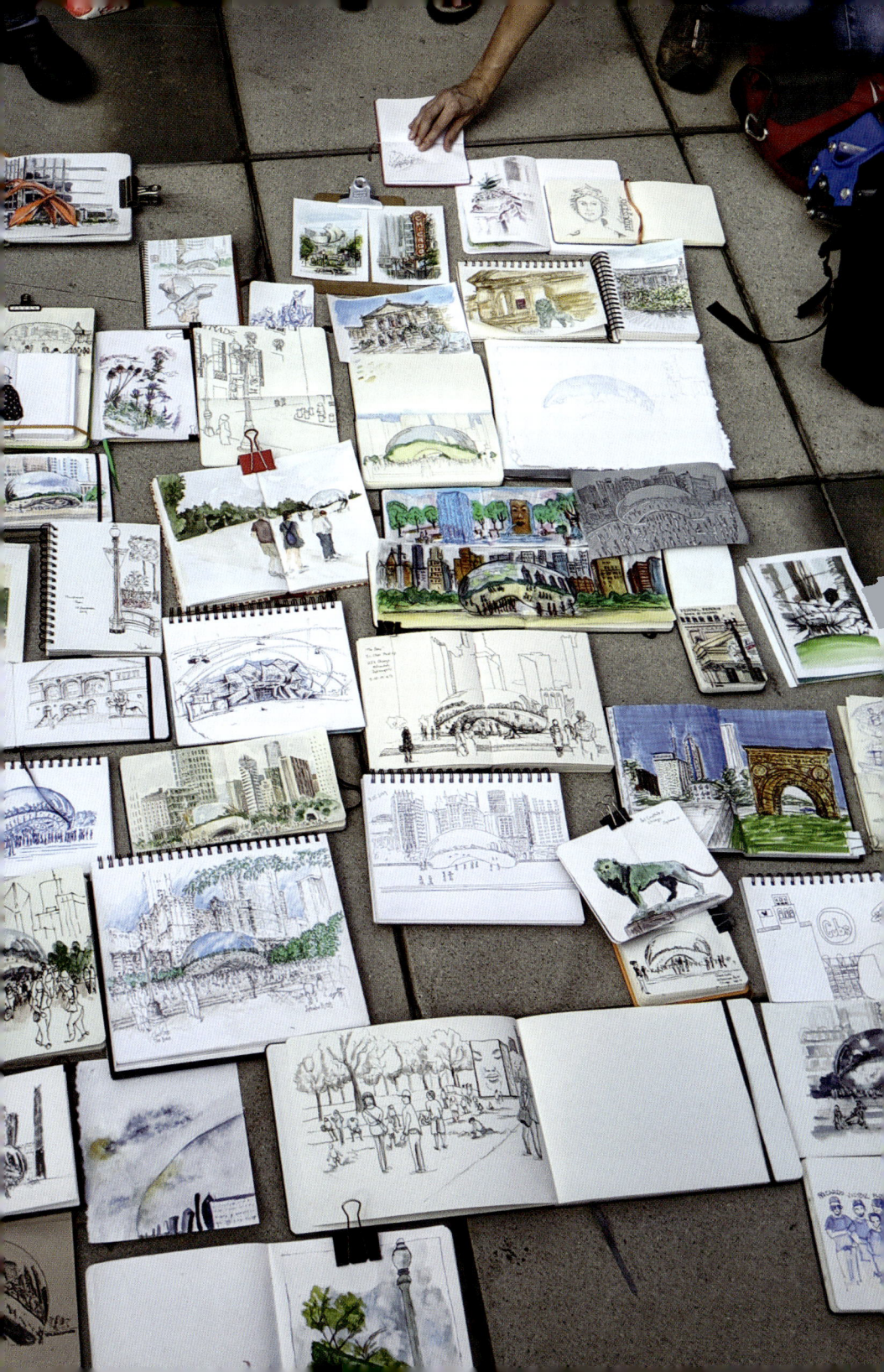

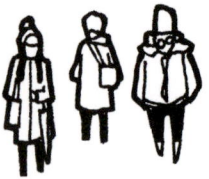

# Teach Others

You may think you have nothing to teach. You may believe you are not good enough. But teaching is not about delivering profound lessons from a higher pedestal. Sometimes the job of teaching is just to pass along good ideas, to share one's discoveries, or to take someone along in your journey. You do not have to position yourself as an expert to do this. People do not always need experts. They need support, and encouragement, and someone with whom to share their interests.

In my experience as a sometimes reluctant teacher, teaching is *useful*. If you think you know something, teach it to someone else. The process of explaining and demonstrating will immediately give you a much deeper understanding.

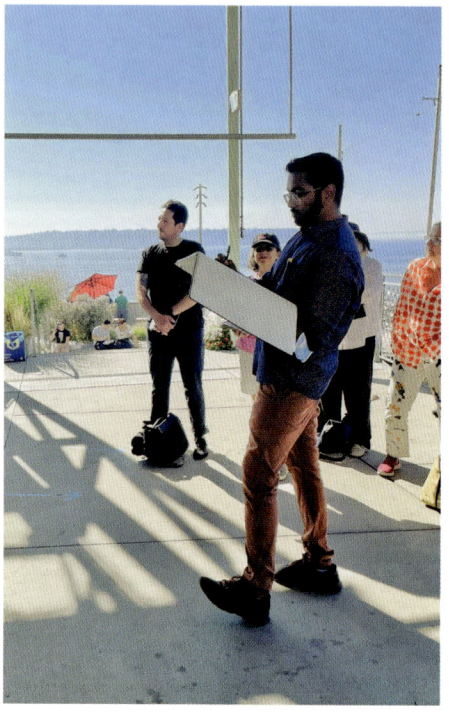

↑ *Teaching a workshop at Seattle's Pike Place Market*

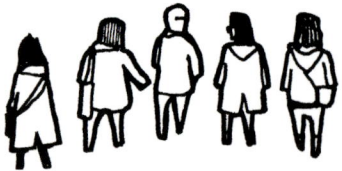

# Be (Un)comfortable

You are on a journey and the path has many peaks and valleys, but one day you may find yourself on a plateau. To keep going on a plateau costs very little energy, but you do not see the gains you used to see in the early days, i.e., when you climbed your first peaks.

You may choose to stay on this course, because it is so comfortable. Drawing within your comfort zone means drawing the things you most enjoy. These things do not intimidate us. They can even help keep our momentum going on days when an art practice feels difficult. A comfort zone can be quite helpful!

But a comfort zone can also be a barrier. And it can become boring. It stops us from meeting fresh challenges. It keeps us from developing new ideas and strategies. It limits our personal growth.

My advice: Get comfortable being uncomfortable. Push at the walls of your comfort zone and grow your world, inch by inch, day after day.

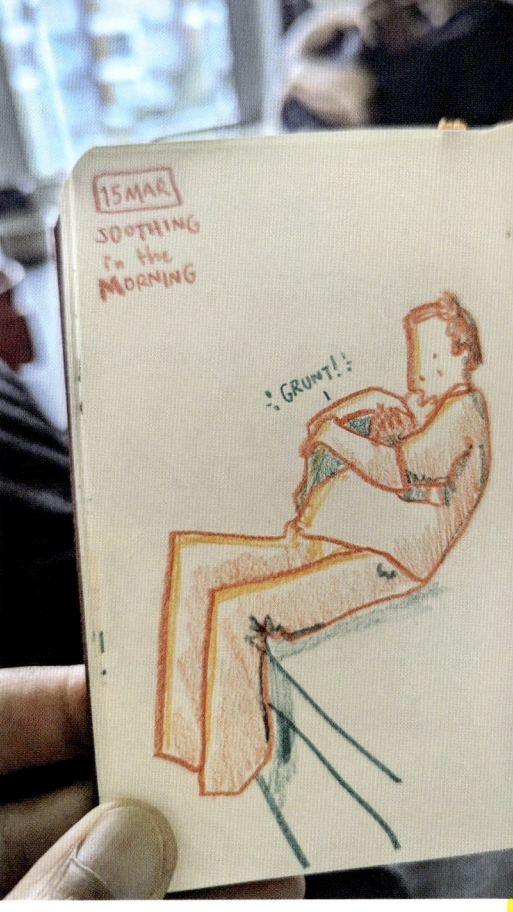

↑ *Challenging myself with colored pencils, to draw my father taking care of my son*

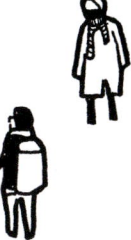

# Be More Human than Ever Before

The practice of art is a deeply human endeavor. These days I meet many people who think the age of human creativity is over. Artificial intelligence will take over all creative work, and human artistry will no longer be needed. Humbly, I disagree.

I think there is a disconnect when we think about the word "art," because immediately it brings up ideas of galleries and auctions and multimillion dollar valuations. Forget the business of fine art. Forget the big numbers. When you sit in a park and express yourself on a sketchbook page, you are not merely drawing at a particular skill level with a particular technique. You are a human experiencing your world and reacting to it with your unique personality, expressing yourself through the many seen and unseen filters of your being.

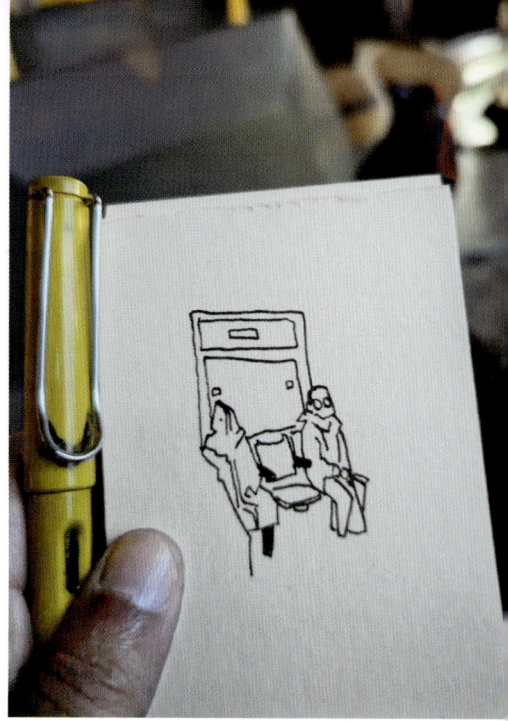

↑ *Being a human observer in my environment*

We are living in a difficult world, in a time of great inhumanity. Make art to reach for something greater than yourself. Make art to compensate for the things you are unable to say. Make art to make this life more bearable. Make art to fill your days with joy. In these times of artificial intelligence, make art to be as intensely human as possible.

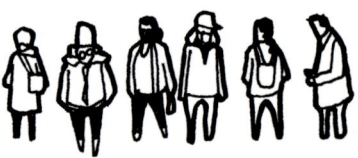

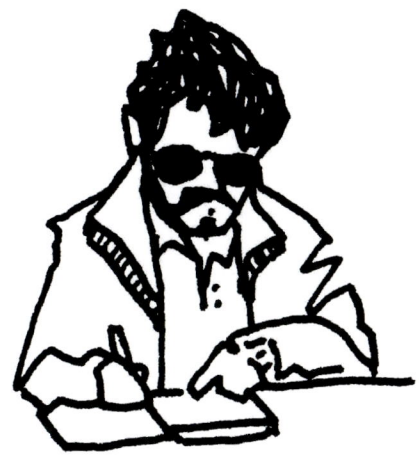

## About the Author

Originally from Kolkata, India, and trained as an engineer, **NISHANT JAIN**
defied expectations and abandoned a PhD in neuroscience to reinvent himself
as an artist, podcaster, and writer. Sneaky Art began as a strategy to circumvent
his anxiety around drawing outdoors, using active observation as a way to learn
to draw. Nishant writes The SneakyArt Post, a weekly newsletter about his art
practice for thousands of readers around the world. His art sells to a growing
global fan base, and he tries to match every sale with a free drawing given away.
He lives in Vancouver, Canada, with his family.

# INDEX

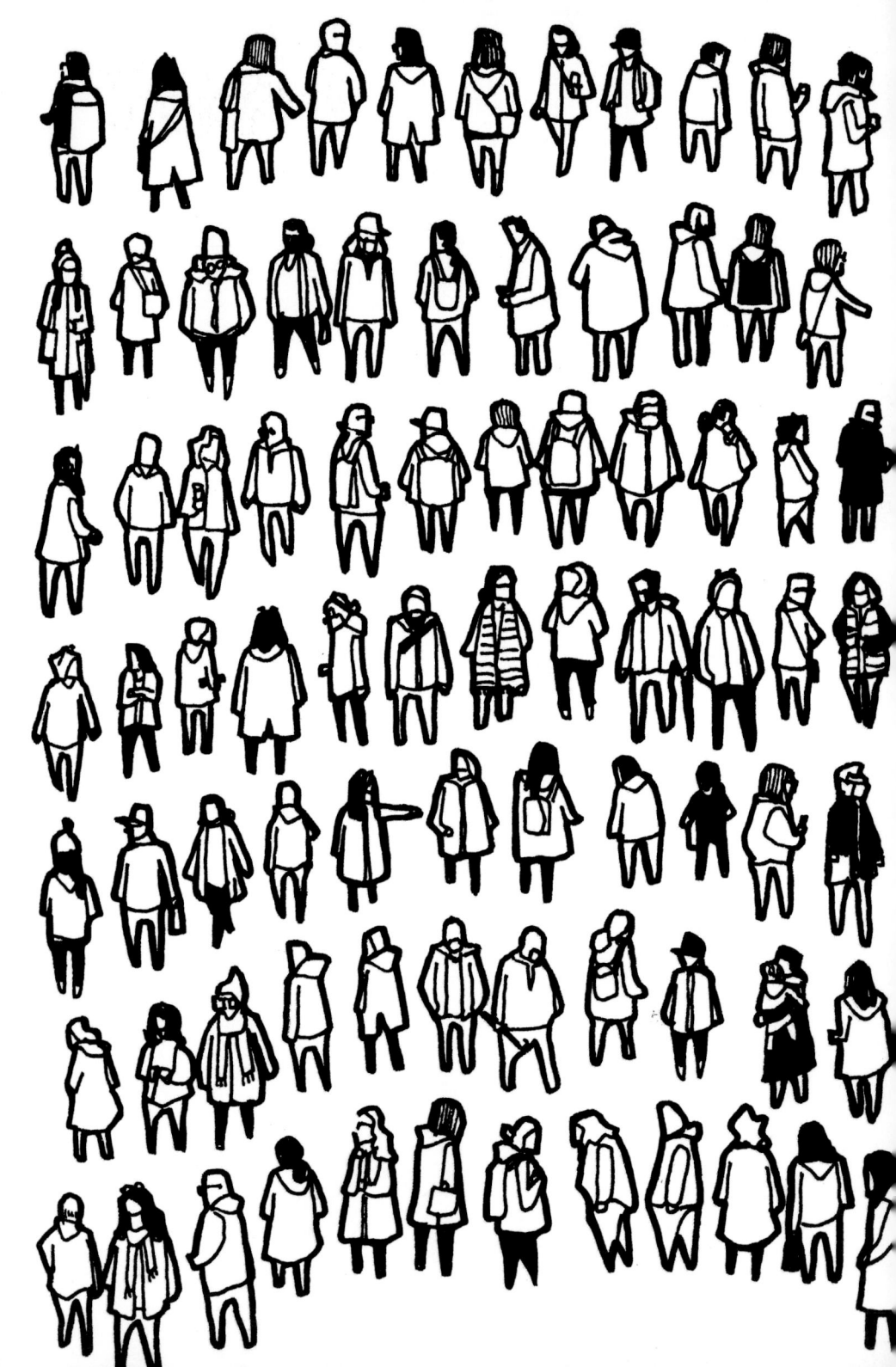